REVIVAL IN ROMANCE
AND REALISM

Tea on the Porch of the Woods' Cottage, Kuling, 1923

Revival In Romance and Realism

By

MRS. HENRY M. WOODS

Founder of the World-Wide Revival Prayer Movement

MARSHALL, MORGAN & SCOTT, LTD.
LONDON :: EDINBURGH

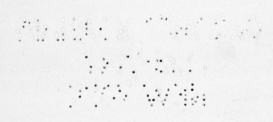

MADE AND PRINTED IN GREAT BRITAIN BY PURNELL AND SONS, LTD.
PAULTON (SOMERSET) AND LONDON

CONTENTS

LIST OF ILLUSTRATIONS

"A BIOGRAPHY OF GOD'S MINISTRY"

"For the true unity of the Spirit is not an edifice to be constructed, but an experience to be declared."

IT is for the purpose of praising the Lord, and to "proclaim his name, and to declare his doings among the people, and to make mention that his name is exalted" that this small volume has been prepared, which testifies to the true unity of the Spirit. There is to-day a mad scramble for so-called "unity," and we hear on every side that, "In unity is strength" (which in some cases is undoubtedly true), but combines of forces do not always *lengthen* the cords and *strengthen* the stakes of God's kingdom. More often than is desirable the cause is weakened rather than strengthened by such a combination.

When we first were made aware that another message from this centre was needed, we saw "men as trees walking," then as the eyes of our understanding were enlightened, touched and illuminated by the Holy Spirit, we began to see more clearly that He had need for the booklet. And the enlightening came through means not anticipated, much less expected. The first was furnished through finding some letters we had thought to be at the bottom of the ocean, for a large box containing correspondence received during our residence in Shanghai had been lost *en route* to the States, somewhere between that

7

city and New York, *via* Indo-China, India, Palestine, Syria, Egypt, Greece, Great Britain, and finally New York, the time element of eight months giving opportunity for the disappearance of much goods. These letters awoke memories which were a prelude to a host of other recollections.

Added to this incentive, the book already partly mapped out, early in February came a letter from that "elect lady," Mrs. A. A. Kirk, of Albany, New York—whose friendship dates over a period of more than thirty-five years and has been most profitable mutually, I trust—who from the first day until now has been a factor in the developments of the Movement. To her intimate friends she is known as "The Encourager," for she has been a succourer to many—the least of these myself also. We here reproduce the words which were like "apples of gold in pictures of silver:"

"Dearest Grace: While there are important letters awaiting, I can hear and see nothing but with your items for the 'new book' you are beginning; a record of the *literature* circulated (of the discovery of the letters she had no knowledge) beginning with *The Half Can Never Be Told*, and going straight on! *Dynamic of Service* occurs to me as next—*Grace Abounding*, *The Wonder of the Book*, and *Hudson Taylor*, etc., etc. Not only the titles, but the extent of the *editions* published and *circulated*. It was reported recently that at Washington, D.C., they have just completed the record of the personnel of Congress! This of itself would be a marvellous biography of God's ministry through you, aside from the regular responsibilities, a record of our 'wonder-working'

God! This urge may seem a little inconsistent, when I am constantly cautioning against excess of activities. But I believe it would work in of itself almost. You have given some of these occasionally in the *Letters*, but a *book* would be a blessed interest to the world constituency—and a *testimony!* A help to generations to come! With each of these publications there could be given *special* testimonies, and you have legions from which to select."

The book as is, by no means gives a full history of the work of "The World-Wide Revival Prayer Movement." Scores of books from the pens of outstanding authors have contributed to the effectiveness of the work so far accomplished, though from the beginning we have focused upon literature bearing directly upon the great and pressing need for Revival. We believe it is profitable that some facts should be known. In his compelling book *Rent Heavens*, a record of the Revival in Wales, the late Rev. R. B. Jones says: "It is right that the facts should be known; more, it is necessary and profitable, God's 'ways' are ever of interest, His 'ways' in Revival especially so; 'ways' that need to be pondered by such as pray for Revival and who might desire to be used in any Revival the future may bring." We trust the facts related herewith may be used for the glory of Him who chooses the weak and foolish things of the world, "that no flesh should glory in his presence." "Because the foolishness of God is wiser than men; and the weakness of God is stronger than men." "We have this treasure in earthen vessels, that the excellency of the power may be of God, and not of us."

Some may find what they consider cause for criticism, but our reluctance to include personal recollections has been overcome through the encouragement of friends who feel that these have a distinct value, and also by the remembrance of an experience related in the biography of a woman who left the stamp of her life upon multitudes. After many years of public service she was called to a more conspicuous work and shrank from the necessary publicity therewith. At last, after much inward struggle with the repeated thought, "But, Lord, the advertising and possible consequent criticism," the Spirit said, "Let them," and all fear fled.

The immortal Bunyan reasoned thus in telling of God's "Grace Abounding" toward himself: "I could also have stepped into a style much higher than this in which I have discoursed, and could have adorned all things more than here I have seemed to do; but I dare not. God did not play in tempting of me; neither did I play, when I sunk as into a bottomless pit, when the pangs of hell caught hold upon me; wherefore, I may not play in relating of them, but be plain and simple, and lay down the thing as it was. He that liketh it, let him receive it; and he that doth not, let him produce a better."

"It is the spirit that quickeneth, the flesh profiteth nothing, the words that I speak unto you, they are spirit and they are life."

May this story of His faithfulness bring life to every reader, for it is the working of His Spirit in the history of His doing that we have been bidden to tell, and which, I need not add, has been personally experienced.

"Blessed is the man that trusteth in the Lord, and whose hope the Lord is. For he shall be as a tree planted by the waters, and that spreadeth out her roots by the river, and shall not see when heat cometh, but her leaf shall be green; and shall not be careful in the year of drought, neither shall cease from yielding fruit" (Jeremiah 17: 7, 8).

> " *The wind that blows can never kill*
> *The tree God plants ;*
> *It bloweth east, it bloweth west,*
> *The tender leaves have little rest,*
> *But any wind that blows is best.*
> *The tree God plants*
> *Strikes deeper root, grows higher still,*
> *Spreads greater boughs, for God's goodwill*
> *Meets all its wants.*
>
> " *There is no storm hath power to blast*
> *The tree God knows ;*
> *No thunderbolt, nor beating rain,*
> *Nor lightning flash, nor hurricane ;*
> *When they are spent, it doth remain.*
> *The tree God knows*
> *Through every tempest standeth fast,*
> *And from its first day to its last*
> *Still fairer grows."*

I

VENTURING FORTH

IT was in 1918, shortly before the Armistice, that I began to set my house in order for flight to a warmer climate during the cold months—where, I did not know. The whole world was at war, and so far as any ordinary mortal could discern, the end was still far distant. It seemed a bad time for planning a journey, indeed, for travel of any kind; but while occupied with necessary preparations, quite without conscious thought my mind was directed toward the Orient—Japan, China, India, Burma—a dream long-cherished. Until this insistent Voice spoke, it had been nothing more than a dream, but the impression deepened until all doubt as to God's call was wiped away.

I announced to my friends, with all assurance, that a trip of this kind was to be undertaken; and then, with as great apparent suddenness as the world was plunged out of war into peace a few days later, I was guided into a new era of my life, for which from earliest childhood I had half-consciously been waiting.

A friend of long standing recently reminded me that many long years ago I told her that I received fifteen missionary periodicals regularly, weekly and monthly, year after year. Almost from a baby I had been familiar with certain missionary efforts. My parents were ardent Baptists, so the story of the heroic, self-sacrificing labours of Adoniram and Ann Judson, those intrepid soldiers of the Cross of Jesus Christ, the work of the Boardmans and others, had been favourite nursery stories. The very first missionary address to which I listened was on the subject of India, a heart-stirring tale of the needs of her teeming millions.

The impression made upon my childish mind was permanent and deep, and though the prospect of a visit to the scenes of the labours of these Crusaders of the Cross was at that time beyond my wildest imaginings, in the fulness of God's time I was actually to tread the same crooked, dusty road over which Adoniram Judson, after weeks and months in one loathsome prison, had been forced to march to another, manacled to a criminal who dropped dead on their weary way. I confess the tears started to my eyes as I too walked that road from Ava to Aungbinle. I felt I was on holy ground. One of the results of that unforeseen visit is a Memorial, in the shape of a restored school and church, to my mother, who told her children of the love of God expressed in His Son Christ Jesus for sinners, and implanted the seeds of real missionary interest in our hearts, to bear fruit after many days.

The beginning of the trip was not easy. Without considering the "lions in the way," I applied for the necessary passport, engaged accommodations, locked the door of No. 5 South Oxford Avenue, Ventnor, N.J., and started north to visit my friends, Dr. and Mrs. Byron Steenberg, of Albany. A letter of credit was waiting for me at Philadelphia, and it was at the bank that I had my first intimation of the difficulties to be overcome. "I suppose you know, Mrs. Taylor," the banker said, "that no passport has been issued to a woman for many months; have you received yours?" I was obliged to confess that this most necessary adjunct was still lacking. "Well," said the gentleman, "I would advise you to leave the letter of credit with us until you receive your passport."

Acting upon this kindly counsel I went my way, with no thought of the long wait before me. As I afterwards reflected upon the inquiry and the finality of the reply, I realized that this gentleman had no expectancy of ever being called upon to deliver the letter of credit.

It was nearly three months before the passport was secured by an act of Providence, a real miracle having been wrought in that connection. At last, however, all was in order, the final good-byes were said, and I started for Vancouver, from whence I sailed in April, 1919.

On the way across the continent I stopped in Chicago to visit a sister who for twenty years was Director of the School of Domestic Arts and Science there. Shortly before leaving her to take the *Empress of Russia* for the voyage across the Pacific, a surprise letter reached me. It was from my brother who was executor of the estate of a sister recently deceased, and contained a cheque for a goodly amount. He explained that some funds had been paid in, and inasmuch as I would be out of the country for a considerable length of time, he felt I was entitled to this advance payment.

I felt very rich with this unexpected amount, and converted it into American Express cheques. On board ship, in the good providence of God, my cabin was directly opposite to that of a family of Southern Baptist missionaries, the Rev. Charles and Mrs.Leonard, and their three children. After the first day at sea I kept to my cabin and did not see the dining-room again until we reached Yokohama, and my neighbours were exceedingly kind and friendly, ministering to my comfort in every possible way. When conditions permitted, either one or the other would come and sit with me and while away the long, tedious hours.

In this way I learned a good deal about conditions in China, and particularly that section in which their own work was located. Mrs. Leonard one day mentioned the pitiful condition of abandoned children there, and the blessing it would mean to have a place in which to care for these waifs. As I thought and prayed about the matter, I came to the conclusion that no better use could be made of the heaven-sent "windfall," so unexpectedly placed in my hands, than to invest a part of it in an orphanage, under Mrs. Leonard's supervision. The amount available would go far toward providing shelter for these pitiful objects of humanity, and before I had reached Yokohama, some of the American Express cheques were in the possession of Mrs. Leonard to be used for this project so much upon her heart. The remaining American Express cheques met a real emergency, but that, as Kipling would say, "is another story"—a very interesting one, I can assure the reader, which may be written at some future time. The friendship cemented during those uncomfortable ten days at sea has strengthened with the years that have followed, and we have never doubted but that our heavenly Father had a care for the orphan children of China when He arranged the location of our cabins on the *Empress of Russia*.

Arriving at Yokohama, I was met by Mr. and Mrs. Gilbert Bowles, or, to use the Friends' "Plain Language," Gilbert Bowles and his wife Minnie Bowles, and was taken to the Friends' Mission Station at Tokyo. "Given to hospitality" is one of the many beautiful features of this home, in which I spent many weeks. In a recent letter Mrs. Bowles says, "I thank God upon every remembrance of you," a statement which strains my credulity; she certainly possesses the charity that covers a multitude of imperfections in others.

After some weeks I went to the great summer resort for missionaries and community people, Karuizawa, and stayed till early autumn. Back in Tokyo, one of the first things to be done was to see our Ambassador to Japan, the Honourable Roland Morris, of Philadelphia. Accompanied by Mrs. Bowles, the call was made shortly before I left Japan for China. The one thing I shall always recall about that day was a question put by the Ambassador when I mentioned my intended extensive itinerary, and that I hoped to visit the Far East before returning to the States. Said Ambassador Morris, "And what are you going to do when you get back, Mrs. Taylor?—write a book?" Without thinking of the absurdity of such an answer, I replied laughingly, "I am going to make a new will!" This was exactly what I did upon reaching Ventnor in the winter of

1921. My new and intimate knowledge of the needs of the missionaries had changed my view-point on many things. I did not think that books were to play so large a part in the programme then beginning for world ministry. A friend wrote during the days of travel, "Your parish, like that of John Wesley, is the world." Later, I was to realize more fully what this meant.

In order to avoid a lengthier ocean trip and also—what was more important—to see as much of missionary work as time permitted, I must needs pass through Korea on the way from Japan to China. Having already twice visited Doshisha University at Kyoto, at the invitation of that "elect lady," Miss Mary Denton, I resisted the temptation of a third visit; and having met Dr. and Mrs. Harry Myers at Karuizawa and at their urgent request paid a visit of some days to Kobe, where 1 was personally conducted through its noisome slums by the now famous Dr. Kagawa, my present intention was to reach Seoul as quickly as possible.

Dr. Robert Hall Glover, Director of North America for the China Inland Mission, was at that time Foreign Missions Secretary of The Christian and Missionary Alliance, and through his good graces I had been furnished with letters of introduction to several missionaries of this mission. Especially eager was I to see the notable work in Shanghai for educated English-speaking Chinese, conducted by the Rev. John and Mrs. Woodberry, and their gifted daughters, Misses Ethel and Ora, a work which while under the auspices of The Christian and Missionary Alliance is in reality, as we have understood, very largely supported by personal friends of the Woodberry family. I lost no time

B

after reaching that city in December, 1919, in making the acquaintance of these good people, so greatly used in reaching young men and women in the quietest, most unobtrusive way.

The Sunday after I arrived I attended a service in the beautiful Christian and Missionary Alliance Chapel, where hundreds of young Chinese men and women had gathered to hear a missionary address from Miss Ruth Paxson on the Home Mission work of the Chinese Church, Miss Paxson having but just returned from a visit to the far-off province of Szechuan. My first stop after leaving Tokyo was at Hiroshima, where the Rev. and Mrs. Lindstrom were in charge of the work, under the auspices of The Christian and Missionary Alliance. It was a most enjoyable and profitable time. After three or four days the journey was resumed, and this time the objective was the famous Leper Colony, founded by Miss Riddell, that notable lady, now gone to her reward, in whose hospitable cottage I had been entertained at Karuizawa during the preceding summer.

While there, Miss Riddell made a proposition that I take charge of the settlement for these sorely afflicted people for six months, while she paid long-deferred visits to the United States and Great Britain in the interests of the work. After due consideration I could only reply that I in no way felt qualified for such responsibility, and therefore could not accept the honour of acting for her in the capacity of friend, counsellor, and guide to the great family, who were daily ministered to with the consideration of honoured guests.

Among other items of interest I learned that friends sometimes contributed a sum of money, sufficient to endow one day in the year with funds to defray the cost of food for all the shutaways. A birthday was usually chosen. This beautiful idea was conceived by one who thought her own deep interest could be extended; and the lepers, in return for the kindness, were pledged to spend some time in prayer for the absent friend. One cannot calculate the effect of such remembrance, sometimes inarticulate because of the loss of features, tongue, or lips, but plainly and clearly understood by Him whose they are, and to whom they are as beloved as any other of His family.

From Kumumoto the path led direct to Seoul. How gladly would I have borrowed the wings of a dove—or even a less attractive bird—to fly from Shimonasaka to Fusan, as nasty a bit of water as the globe holds; but being denied this blessing I simply resigned myself to the misery of seasickness for the next twelve hours.

It was the morning after reaching the fascinating city of Seoul, and while out seeing something of that ancient city with my gracious hostess, Mrs. Bliss Billings, that the again-arresting Voice bade me cancel the passage to India. At once I informed friends at home of the altered plans, instructions having already been forwarded regarding mailing address in India, etc., and then I waited to see what He would say as to the "nexte thynge."

At the end of seven years, when travelling days were past, I could say out of a full heart, "The lines have fallen unto me in pleasant places," and one of the pleasantest places was this home of Dr. and Mrs. Bliss Billings, missionaries of the Methodist Episcopal

Church at Seoul, and though I cannot recall the name of the angel who guided me to this altogether delightful bailiwick, I have no difficulty in remembering the great kindness these new friends showed me on the occasions that it was my very great good fortune to be entertained in their home, both in coming to Japan in 1919 and going back there in 1920.

After several days with these kind hosts I continued my journey, stopping *en route* at Shanghai by invitation to visit several mission stations and get acquainted with the various activities of the different denominations, for I had no predilection for any one enterprise: all mission work was equally near the heart. On arrival at Shanghai, I made my home with the ladies of "The Door of Hope."

Two incidents—or events, as one chooses to look at these things—in connection with this visit stand out in bold relief. The first was that of a girl rescued a very short while before, a pitiable object, so recently snatched from the snare of the fowler that she was still contrasting the present love and friendliness of her new surroundings with the shame which had cut into the very marrow of her being. In telling her story she would describe the manner of bartering that entered into the selling of her body and soul, and always with a voice lowered to a whisper when she came to the last words: "I was weighed, just like a pig."

The other occurrence that made a lasting impression was a planned break for liberty. A number of girls chose Sunday evening to escape, hiding in ash-cans, but were discovered before their plans were carried out. Perhaps this would long ago have been forgotten, but it happened that the "inquiry room" was located next to the room I occupied, and voices were perfectly distinct. Miss Morris had been chosen to use the knife as soul-surgeon in the difficult task of readjustment to the former good and regular standing in the big family of one and another of the culprits. She sought to show each one who entered the room the error of her way. There was not a single word of scolding, but a patient pointing out of the wrong, first to themselves and then to the Home. The gentle probing brought the truth to the surface, and one and another with confession, weeping, and prayer, were reinstated.

"The Door of Hope" in Shanghai is an outstanding monument to God's guidance and provision. "God's work done in God's way will never lack for any good thing" is pre-eminently true of this shelter for the helpless and homeless. Nearly every girl and woman who enters there becomes a truly born-again soul. The reputation of its inmates is known throughout China, and eligible young men seek their helpmeets from this centre—indeed, the supply is far below the demand in this respect, we have been told.

Soon after the New Year I went to the Philippine Islands for some weeks, among other things to visit the school and evangelistic work of The Christian and Missionary Alliance at Zamboanga, ably conducted by Mrs. Lund, during her husband's absence in the States. I therefore did not return to China until early spring.

II

TRAVELLING MERCIES

IN the summer of 1920 the controversy between Fundamentalism and Modernism reached its climax, and nowhere more sharply than in China. Returning in May from the Philippines, I had been invited to visit the missions in Ningpo, Hangkow, and other interior stations; and when the hot weather came I went to Kuling, the largest mountain resort for both foreigners and Chinese. Here I was a paying guest at The Quakerage, Miss Esther Butler, head of the Friend's Work in Nanking, having invited me to become a member of her family. Included in this privilege was the saintly Miss Margaret Holme, a member of the Mission having an evangelistic work at Luho, some two or more miles trom Nanking. As I was afterward to learn, a family by the name of Woods, a father and two daughters, was also among the summer cottagers, and it was during the following weeks that the troubled meetings were held.

Dr. Griffith Thomas and Dr. Charles G. Trumbull were the special speakers, imported by the "Milton Stewart Evangelistic Committee," and their presence brought things to a crisis. Meetings were held almost daily, with the result that a cleavage, deep and wide, was made between the two factions. A Bible Union for China was formed. From that day to this there has been a determined effort "to cleanse the inside of the cup," as well as polish the outside of the platter, and the present controversy between Fundamentalists and Modernists threatens to disrupt the smooth-running machinery of the ecclesiastical hierarchy. How rapidly all these differences would disappear under the beneficent influence of a heaven-sent revival! Like the Prophet Isaiah, men would be crying out: "Woe is me! for I am undone, because I am a man of unclean lips, and I dwell in the midst of a people of unclean lips: for mine eyes have seen the King, the Lord of Hosts." Oh! that an angel might touch our lips with a live coal from off the altar, then should all iniquity cease and God would be glorified in all the members of His Body, of which Jesus Christ is the glorious Head.

A stranger in a strange land, I was, nevertheless, deeply interested in the trend of events, and attended meetings open to all and sundry. In the drama being enacted, Dr. Henry M. Woods, a missionary under the Southern Presbyterian Board, was "chief among the brethren." During these meetings we must have seen each other many times, though I was all unconscious of the contacts. Not so the gentleman in question. He seems to have a very vivid recollection of these one-sided meetings, for he recalls time after time when we not only met but actually exchanged words. In an effort to stimulate remembrance, Dr. Woods later wrote: "My memory is better than yours. I remember every time I saw you. Perhaps it is not that my memory is better, but that I had an object more worthy of remembrance."

Of these memorable meetings I have no recollection, and it was not until shortly after my return to
the little home at Ventnor, early in the winter of 1921,
that I became aware that such a person existed.
Very soon I began receiving letters postmarked Soochow, China, and was not a little mystified as to the
identity of the writer. The contents revealed that
which was so obscure to my unimaginative mind.
The basis of interest centred around the Bible Union
and its development. I reasoned that the writer
was a kindly person who, feeling deeply the principle
involved, was reaching out to interest home friends.
The letters continued to come with regularity, although my replies were infrequent and founded solely
upon the work vital to both of us. Finally, just
before leaving home again the next summer for the
deferred trip to Burma and India, a contribution to
the work of the Bible Union was sent, and I supposed
that this would close the correspondence. But in
this supposition I erred, for letters continued to follow all along the way.

Little did I dream, when the shores of my native
land receded into dim outlines and then were completely lost, that August day in 1921, that it would be
five full years before my eyes would rest again upon
the beloved States. My friend, Mrs. A. A. Kirk, of
Albany, who had been Dean of Women at the Bible
Institute at Nyack, N.Y., during the days of Dr.
Simpson's world-wide activities, was accompanying
me as far as England. After some weeks in London
together, I said good-bye to her, and went on my way
to Paris, stopped at several cities in Italy, and in

DR. AND MRS. WOODS EXAMINING CHINESE BIBLE AND
ENCYCLOPAEDIA

THE FIVE WOODBERRYS, AS THEY LOOKED IN SEPTEMBER, 1925,
WITH "KATHERINE," THEN TWO YEARS OLD

[Face page 24

November sailed from Brindisi for Alexandria, where I remained till late December, reaching Bombay just before the holiday season.

Having at last reached the land of ardent desire, India, I found myself with an embarrassment of riches in the form of delightful cards of all descriptions, which had been sent in care of "Cook's," the American Express Company, and the Consulates, both British and American.

It was obviously my duty to thank the kind sender. From that time the die was cast, which was to unite our forces for the Kingdom interests. Before I left India, or rather Ceylon, for China in the early spring of 1923, the great question had been asked and answered, and I had the distinction of being that rare creature, a woman who had accepted a man she had, as far as she could remember, never seen, but, please remember, he was a missionary! He had, however, sent me his photograph! And on April 6 of that year, Henry M. Woods and Grace W. Taylor were united in marriage at the home of Dr. and Mrs. S. I. Woodbridge in Shanghai, Dr. Woodbridge performing the ceremony, an act which two years later he reported to Mrs. Sampson, Dr. Woods' sister, as "the best missionary work of all my long years in China."

It was many moons after our first meeting at Kuling in the summer of 1920 that I learned this interesting detail in the process that led to our union: when from the register—a close watch having been kept on that telltale book—Dr. Woods discovered that coolies and a chair had been booked for my descent of the mountain on a certain day, he also discovered that important

business would need his immediate presence in Shanghai, strangely enough to coincide with my expected
arrival. Reaching Shanghai, he made his way to the
Missionary Home, to find, with no little disappointment, that the object of his quest had not arrived
there, and forthwith there followed a round of all the
hotels and paying guest-houses in the city in the hope,
vain though it proved to be, of discovering my whereabouts.

What had happened was, I might say parathetic-
ally, that upon reaching Kiukiang, the city at the
base of Kuling, I had accompanied missionaries of
the Brethren's Mission to the ancient city of Nanchang, where they carry on a vigorous and fruitful
evangelistic work in the midst of scenes made famous
by the great traveller and explorer, Marco Polo.
The city at the time of my visit was practically unchanged from the days of the Thirteenth Century, the
only means of travel, except by foot, being the wheel-
barrow. Now we learn that a modern up-to-date
hotel has been built, a frequent indication of the new
China and her progress to-day.

While in Nanchang I was a guest in the home of Mr.
and Mrs. F. H. Hopkins, and the story of their call is
an interesting one, and of value in a missionary
chronicle such as this. Some years before this time
they had burned their bridges behind them and set
out for China to join the colony of missionaries at
Nanchang, among whom were Mr. Kingsbury, Mrs.
Hopkins' brother, his wife and their two little girls.
Mr. Hopkins had left an important post as a civil
engineer to respond to the Lord's "Go ye." It was

while Mr. and Mrs. Hopkins were *en route* from England to China, five days out from Southampton, that the news reached them of the tragic deaths of Mr. Kingsbury, Mrs. Kingsbury, and one of their children, all of whom had been brutally murdered during a disturbance with which they were in no way connected. To turn back would have been the natural reaction, but this did not enter the minds of these intrepid soldiers of the Cross. Much prayer was made during the remainder of the journey, and one petition went up from their hearts daily, "Lord, we are willing to serve Thee in China; only do not ask that we go to Nanchang."

Reaching Shanghai, they found friends had come to meet them, and it was not long before the question came, "Will you return with us to Nanchang?" This was the crucial test of faith, but by His grace they were enabled to take up the cross and fill the gap made vacant by the sudden Home-call of their loved ones.

Upon returning to Shanghai late in that September of 1920 from Nanchang, I began preparations for the trip, to be taken leisurely, up through Peking, *via* Manchuria, to Yokohama, from which port I had engaged passage to the States. While at supper one evening, soon after reaching the Missionary Home in Shanghai, the superintendent brought to our table a gentleman who had just arrived, and introduced him as Mr. G—— from South Africa. He told us something of the details of his journey. Many weeks before he had started on his long journey, the objective being the World's Sunday School Convention then in session at Tokyo, Japan. Delays, a shipwreck among others, had prevented his reaching Shanghai earlier, and now he learned that there would be no sailing before three days, which would not allow him time to reach Tokyo before the close of the Convention. As we listened—especially since he said he had been appointed delegate of the missionary body in his part of South Africa to bring back a report of Convention doings—we began to think of a way by which he could get there. The overland journey was mentioned, which he hadn't known existed, but his seeming reluctance to commit himself puzzled us. After supper when a little group gathered around him to talk further about his getting to Tokyo in time, he reluctantly confessed that he had not enough money left, after all his unexpected delays, to finance the overland trip. In order to take the journey at all, the second of two furloughs in forty years, he had had to draw on his life insurance.

Assuring him that in some way or other the Lord would provide, the little group dispersed. At ten o'clock that evening, passing through the drawing-room, we found him calmly reading a book, so we knew he had cast his care upon the Lord. A little later two of the women of the party, one the Superintendent of the Home, made their way to the Railroad Station and when they came back they had a through ticket to Tokyo with them.

Mr. G—— reached the Convention three days before the close, and was providentially brought into immediate contact with Dr. Charles G. Trumbull, editor of the *Sunday School Times* and one of the chief speakers; through him he was put into touch with leaders from many parts of the world, and, as he afterwards wrote from South Africa, was able to take back a full report of the entire eight days of the great gathering, with immensely helpful results.

Dr. Woods, at the time of our marriage in 1923, was in the midst of his work of four big volumes, *The Chinese Bible Encyclopedia*, in Chinese, and, after spending the summer in Kuling, we moved to Shanghai in the fall to be near the great Commercial Press where the printing of the Encyclopedia was to be done, and where the possibilities were better for securing the necessary help of qualified Chinese scholars. The most particular work yet to be done was the assembling of the articles which had been scattered throughout home and foreign periodicals, and at least the end seemed in sight, though not very near. The work had been in progress since the summer of 1919. It is said that "Coming events cast their shadows before them," but in this case the "shadow" had failed to appear, or I had failed to recognize it, for I was wholly unprepared for the long delay that stretched before us; the finishing of the Encyclopedia was to open the way for an early return to the States. Dr. Woods had written some time before I left India:

"Don't delay coming on account of the Encyclopedia, as it cannot be finished before June at the earliest; some influential Chinese friends who are helping a little, but cannot give all their time to it, say it will take longer time than that, as there is so much to review. I know, perhaps, how you feel about going to the U.S.A., for, while I love China and the work here and appreciate the many blessings and enjoyable things we have here, one can never have the same feeling that you have towards our native land. There is a tug at the heart whenever you see the old flag or anything connected with the U.S.A."

Like Joseph we were to learn that the seeming "evil" was meant of God for good, for all this time He was working out His purpose to prove us, knowing what He would do. But for this long drawn-out delay, there would have been no prayer meeting on January 1, 1924, with its far-reaching influence and almost unthinkable results, followed by the Shanghai Revival, that "gracious and glorious work of the Holy Spirit," from which the record, *The Half Can Never Be Told*, was written, which has inspired thousands to pray for a great Awakening throughout the whole world—"That men may know that thou, whose name alone is Jehovah, art the most high over all the earth." That has been followed by other books—all pointing to the work and ministry of the Holy Spirit, the representative of the Godhead here upon earth—which to-day have been the means of creating a great volume of intercessory prayer. By night and day saints are pleading with the Almighty; in deep reverence it may be said that "they give Him no rest," until Jerusalem shall be made a praise upon the earth.

June and the "longer time" had passed. October had arrived and the "deadline" crossed for our return to the States and waiting business affairs. These we had left in trust upon our God, but various stories related, of sudden losses and dishonesty of trustees, made me anxious as I was so far from home.

An incident related by one of the guests at a dinner in our home, one evening, did not tend to tranquilize the mind. This lady had been a travelling companion to the friend whose sad experience she related. Both ladies were ardent admirers and staunch supporters of Foreign Missionary work. In due time it came about they were in a position to visit the places that had caught at their heart, and unloosed their purse-strings —and they set sail for the great land of China, with the thought of seeing many of the China Inland Mission stations.

Dr. M—— had, with perfect confidence in the integrity of the man who had looked after her financial interests for many years, placed practically all her earthly possessions in his hands. After some months of travel, having fulfilled the mission on which they were bent, they returned to the States. Dismay and distress seized the lady, when she discovered that the man she had trusted with her earthly goods had betrayed his trust to enrich himself, squandering her fortune in riotous living. Had not her mission been undertaken in the full belief that it was according to the will of the Lord? How then could she reconcile this terrible thing with the faith exercised? She brooded over the situation, her mind travelling round and round in unrest, terror, unhappiness, turning this problem over and over in her mind, until she became mentally unbalanced, a condition which lasted over a period of several years. My feelings during the recital of this appalling story may be better imagined than described, for it was a counterpart of the first part of my own experience. However, I soon recovered from the waking nightmare, for upon calm reflection I was more than ever certain that the words: "He that followeth me shall not walk in darkness, but shall have the light of life" (John 8 : 12), had been, were being, and would be fulfilled.

Casting about in my mind for someone to "take hold of His Covenant" with me for protection of property and deliverance from distress of mind, the Holy Spirit directed my thoughts to Miss Gertrude Metcalf, head of the Christian's Mission, Ningpo, who happened (?) to be in Shanghai at this crucial time. In her I found an understanding heart, and a solemn covenant was entered into to claim the promise: "If two of you shall agree on earth as touching any thing that they shall ask, it shall be done for them of my Father which is in heaven." And He who has promised that not a sparrow shall fall to the ground without His knowledge, faithfully preserved every penny of that which He had committed to our stewardship. How needful it is that God's people should recognize that we are not our own, nor anything that we possess. It is ours only as loaned for His use. May we be found faithful in the discharge of our stewardship!

How wonderfully our God undertook may be gathered from one instance. The young Jewish woman who had been in our attorney's employ for many years visited me, at my request, after our return in 1926. I had brought a small gift for her as I had many times seen her when I called at the office on business. As we chatted for a few minutes, I said, "It seems perfectly wonderful that Mr. C——— has been able to account for every penny of the money left in his care." With a sharp intake of breath, Miss A——— replied, "And don't I know it! I had to make up the accounts when you were expected, and he kept me looking two whole weeks for TWO CENTS!"

Trust in the Lord is never violated nor betrayed. While on our missionary journey, we were told of a godly man, active in the work of the Lord, a contributor to every good work, who lost his fortune through faith in a friend whom he trusted implicitly. After the story was told, came the question, "How do you account for such a thing? Does not the first Psalm say: 'Blessed is the man whose delight is in the law of the Lord . . . and whatsoever he doeth shall prosper!'" The line between faith and presumption is thin. We cannot hold God accountable nor His Word untrue when we assume that a thing that looks good *is* good; to "try the spirits" is the only safety for the child of God. When circumstances over which we have no control, as in the case of my own affairs, must be met, we can certainly ask HIM to rule and overrule to His glory. To assume, because we bear the name of Christian, that therefore God must stamp with approval every act we commit and all service we render in His Name, is to miss the mark, and it accounts for the wreckage of countless lives and the loss of service for His eternal glory. "He that searcheth the hearts knoweth the mind of the Spirit." "All things work together for good to them that love

c

God, to them who are the called according to his purpose."

A favourite diversion from the arduous and difficult task of completing the Encyclopedia—a truly monumental task needing the greatest amount of concentration of mind—was collecting rare and sometimes priceless porcelain pieces for our hoped-for home. The old city of Soochow is a perfect Mecca for collectors of such objects, and long residence in China, such as my husband had had, with a natural love of the beautiful, had developed a sense of values not to be absorbed quickly. One of many such pieces, acquired early and kept for nearly three years before bestowal, is a blue-and-white vase of exquisite shape and colouring, so unusual that it is thought to have been the property of a royal personage; it is the only one of the kind known to be in existence. This is among the most cherished of our possessions and never fails to elicit Ohs! and Ahs! when shown to friends who have a knowledge of the beautiful in Chinese *objets d'art*.

An instance of how God answered prayer in the matter of a much needed qualified Chinese scholar for the Encyclopedia work is memorable. Mr. Edgar Strother called one day when we were concerned for the speeding up of the work, for we had planned to return to the United States a few months after our marriage. Weeks had lengthened into months, during which time we had waited none too patiently, I fear, to see the end, but all the time God was working out His purpose, as will be seen later in this narrative. We mentioned to Mr. Strother the need for a specially prepared Chinese, for the difficult work of translating some articles written in the United States. He seemed to regard the matter as rather dubious, but promised to be on the look-out for such a paragon. Within a very few days, a deeply spiritual and highly educated Chinese gentleman from a distant province walked into the office of the Christian Endeavour Society, which Mr. Strother and his wife represented in China at that time. After a little conversation, the subject of the Encyclopedia was broached. To Mr. Strother's surprise this gentleman seemed very willing to consider the proposition, and at once paid Dr. Woods a call. Being found well adapted to the work, he was engaged and proved an invaluable addition to the staff of workers.

When leaving home in the summer of 1921, we had thought to be absent not more than two years. "Whatsoever is not of faith is sin," and we felt that "faith" had been vouchsafed for an absence of this duration,' and now we were being held in China far beyond the period planned, as we thought at the time, to be in the will of God. There is a sense in which we are to take no thought for the morrow. And there is another sense when we are to take every precaution to conserve for the future the interests of that which affects the Kingdom. This was our concern. Meanwhile, much suffering was my lot. From the day of my arrival in China, repeated attacks of 'flu, acute indigestion and other ailments left me an easy prey to all sorts of ills. Last of all, typhoid fever, with relapse after relapse, reduced the remaining strength of body.

During the days of convalescence after one such seizure, "Memory's cold storage" furnished refreshment with a bit from C. H. Spurgeon's *Morning and*

Evening Daily Readings. This most helpful devotional book had been given me many years before, but with many changes and travels I had entirely lost track of my valued little volume, worn from much use. Pleasant recollections of various themes made me long to obtain another copy. The one I had was purchased in the States, but we believed it was published in Britain, but where and by whom was the question. After praying that we might be able to obtain another copy, we left the matter with our Lord. At Christmas I received the book I so desired, a gift from a British lady, a friend whom I had met at Kashmir. It was posted at the very time we had prayed for it to come our way. Some years later we made a distribution of this book to Theological and Bible Students—a goodly number of copies reached missionaries on the field— and all greatly prized the gift. From the student at Princeton, now Rev. Frank Faucette, who was responsible for its distribution there, we heard that one of the little red books was to be seen by the bedside of almost every student, showing its real appreciation in its constant use. And the Rev. Paul Harrison, one of the faculty at The Evangelical Theological College in Dallas, was as enthusiastic in his expression of appreciation of this grant, as were many others.

Our enforced stay in China was not without many compensations. Not the least of these was the comfort and pleasure derived from knowing that the home at 5 South Oxford Avenue, Ventnor, N.J., was in good hands; for it was occupied by no less a person than Mrs. John Russell Sampson, the only sister of my husband. Having disposed of her own home in Richmond,

Virginia, she had for some time made her headquarters with a missionary daughter, Mrs. Richard V. Taylor, at Rochester, Minnesota. When the time came for Dr. and Mrs. Taylor and their family to return to their work in China, Mrs. Sampson was cut adrift. The home of her younger daughter in Denver was not suitable for her, Mrs. Sampson having a heart condition not equal to living at that high altitude. Coming East, she tried to be contented at a sanatorium, and this seemed the logical solution for her dilemma in her indifferent health. But she was becoming uneasy there, as we learned through frequent letters, and we conceived the idea of offering her 5 South Oxford Avenue. It was promptly accepted. She moved in with the assistance of interested friends, the Hon. John Wanamaker among others. Strangely enough, as soon as her wonderful powers had scope for action, she recovered her health so fully that the house was filled with grateful guests, literally from garret to cellar. Relatives and friends were legion, and she enjoyed a reputation as hostess second to none.

From "The House Beautiful," as Mrs. Sampson called the very modest dwelling, she wrote hundreds of letters, and we think it will add interest to this narrative to quote from two or three:

"I feel that it is not wise to get anything in the way of clothing I can possibly do without—in view of my possibly 'slipping awa'' any day. That prospect is lessened since coming here, for though still lame (and always must be) and full of aches, I am so much better. You did not mean to keep me out of heaven a long time; did you? It is a disappointment to me, but the comfort is, as in everything, that God knows and chooses for us as we would choose for ourselves if we knew as much as He does. He certainly plans wonderful things for us. I never could have dreamed of such a thing as this house and all it has been to so many this summer."

At another time:

"Your letter received to-day found me very happy in this lovely home of yours. Dear sister, certainly your loving-kindnesses are like the Lord's own and 'fail not.' I was delighted with the charming tea-cloth and lovely doilies; there was no duty to pay, so your thoughtfulness was not needed. I love the Chinese linens and their work. I am sending you a lot of family letters, again; since you are a Woods now, I know you are discreet. These show you the real folks and make you better acquainted than weeks in the home with them. All the ties of blood mean much to me; yet I feel as near to you as if you had been born my sister. It is not to be wondered at that Henry calls you 'Dorothy,' for you are indeed a 'gift of God' to him and his family."

After Mrs. Sampson left Ventnor and returned to Richmond, her former home town, she wrote:

"I am visiting in the home of M. T., who asked for the loan of your photograph to take to her Sunday-school class of girls. The lesson was on Philippians 4, and she wished to illustrate verse 8: 'Finally, whatsoever things are true, whatsoever things are honest, whatsoever things are just, whatsoever things are pure, whatsoever things are lovely, whatsoever things are of good report; if there be any virtue and if there be any praise, think on these things,' as it shows what such thinking will produce in the countenance."

This was one of the finest compliments one could receive.

The Encyclopedia was completed in 1925. How well this monumental and important work was received is shown by the following quotation:

"Information comes to the Presbyterian Committee of Publication that there is a big demand for the *Chinese Encyclopedia* which is being prepared by Dr. Henry M. Woods. A letter from Mrs. Woods reads: 'Exceeding abundantly above! The 4,000 sets first edition sold! Orders nearing the 5,000 mark. Our concern now is how to meet the demand. The book will not be off the press for some weeks yet (letter written Feb. 27). My husband can hardly realize the wonder of it all.' "

The Rev. Edward Mack, D.D., Professor of Old Testament Literature, Union Theological Seminary, Richmond, Virginia, visited Japan and China in the summer of 1925, and his appreciation of the work just completed appeared in one of the Southern Presbyterian Church papers under the heading of "The Chinese Encyclopedia of the Bible":

"A work of exceeding interest and of the greatest importance has just been issued from the press in China. This valuable publication is *The Bible Encyclopedia for the Chinese Church*, which has been prepared under the direction, and largely by the personal efforts of the

Rev. Henry M. Woods, D.D.   Most of the material for it was translated by permission of the respective publishers of conservative Bible dictionaries and encyclopedias in the English language, some notable articles were prepared by scholars in China, America and other countries; and to these latter credit has been given in the index section of the work. A large part of the material was translated from the International Standard Bible Encyclopedia, published some years ago by the Howard-Severance Company, under the editorial direction of the late Dr. James Orr.

"The publication of this work in China marks an epoch of progress in the missionary work in that land, and at the same time makes provision for Christian education through able and authoritative Christian literature. Unfortunately, too large a portion of the working and reference literature of the young Chinese Church has been taken from liberal and radical sources, to which unfortunate condition much of the liberalism which marks and mars the Chinese Church has been due. All the Christian world will welcome the publication of this great conservative body of Bible literature and its availability for all the Christian schools and communions of China.

"The work has been published in four handsomely bound and splendidly printed volumes. At the same time the purchase price has been made so low that it is placed within the reach of every Christian minister and theological student in Chinese schools and churches. The set was sold at the low introductory price of $2.50 Mexican money, and I have been informed that theological students were able to buy the set even at a discount on this incredibly low purchase price. This wonderfully small cost is not due so much to the low price of the manual labour involved in publication in

China, as to the devotion and liberality of Dr. and Mrs. Woods, and to contributions made largely through a special committee of the Synod of Virginia.

"In his quiet, gentle and unassuming way Dr. Woods has devoted his great ability and wide scholarship to the rendering of a noble service to China and the whole Christian world. One can confidently predict for this great work a run of many editions in the coming years. For all who are interested in conservative Christian scholarship and earnest evangelistic effort in China I can confidently voice unanimous expression of gratitude to Dr. Woods, for the talented, arduous and patient service, which has brought so rich a gift to Christ and the kingdom in China."

We finally reached Ventnor, August, 1926, after eight months of continuous travelling from the time we left Shanghai; for since his student days in Edinburgh my husband has cherished the hope of one day going around the world. Long before we reached home, however, I realized more fully God's purpose in detaining us. Not only was the Chinese Bible Encyclopedia completed, but the World-Wide Revival Movement was "brought to the birth" and the Shanghai Revival had become a matter of history.

III

FURTHER PREPARATIONS

IT was at a prayer meeting held on New Year's Day, 1924, in Shanghai, that the World-Wide Revival Prayer Movement was born. It came about in this way. On the second Sunday in December we had two notable speakers at the Free Christian Church—Mr. George T. B. Davis at the morning service and Mr. Charles Rankin at the evening service. Mr. Davis was on his way from Australia, where he had spent more than a year in evangelistic work, including the distribution of many New Testaments, to do much the same work in the great army of General Feng, the so-called "Christian General," which was stationed near Peking. It was something that Mr. Rankin—a lawyer by profession, a missionary by preference—had said about the terrible condition of the lost (his sermon was on Dives and Lazarus) that brought to a focus thoughts that had been occupying my mind for years, and especially since the extensive travels which had covered more than four years in foreign countries.

In the days following I could think of little else than the words spoken that Sunday evening, and the determination grew to extend an invitation to a prayer meeting to pray for world-wide revival. On Sunday, December 23, we had Mr. Davis and Mr. Rankin as our dinner-guests, and the concern felt was expressed to Mr. Davis especially, as he was a veteran in Christian work, having travelled with Chapman and Alexander on their wide evangelistic campaigns. He expressed the keenest interest in the proposed prayer meeting and consented to be present, provided he and his mother were still in Shanghai at the time we proposed calling together the friends for prayer.

Having this encouragement, we sent out twenty or more invitations, and if the action had been concerted it could not have been with greater unanimity, for all with one consent begged to be excused, "a previous engagement" given as the reason in almost every instance. The Sunday before the appointed day an effort was made by some to have the date changed to a more convenient season. This we could not see to be that which He had shown as His time, and remembering that His Word says that, "Where two or three are gathered together in my name, there am I in the midst," and having learned that "One with God is a majority," the matter was left as planned. The next morning, as I stopped at the Missionary Home for some now-forgotten reason, I ran into Miss Paxson, and her first words after exchanging greetings were, "I am coming to your house to-morrow." Surprised, I said, "But I thought you had an engagement for Tuesday." "I did have; but the prayer meeting is more important, so the other has been cancelled." This incident is indicative of the opposition that the adversary has manifested to this work from the very beginning, and his defeats have followed in regular sequence. Not only did Miss Paxson and her colleague, Miss Davis, cancel what were considered important previous invitations, but with the exception of possibly two or three of those approached in the matter, all arrived on schedule time on the afternoon of January 1, 1924.

Mr. Davis spoke briefly, and then I told of the concern which weighed upon my spirit for the souls for whom Christ had paid the penalty of their sins on the Cross of Calvary. There was scarcely any discussion, but we all knelt before Him to offer our petitions and listen for anything He might have to say to us. It was a real meeting for prayer, and the covering of the Spirit was manifested to all. After we rose from our knees, Miss Jennie Hughes voiced the thought occupying more than one mind, that this should continue; and a committee composed of Drs. Lowrie, Bryan, Woodbridge, Woods, Dr. Dora Yu, Miss Hughes, myself, and, later, Mr. D. E. Hoste, General Director of the China Inland Mission, and Miss Ruth Paxson, was formed to further the work of the Holy Spirit in prayer and intercession for revival in the Body of Christ and the salvation of sinners. It was suggested that Mrs. Woods act as Chairman and, though protest was made, principally on the ground of the near (?) approach of furlough, the majority carried their point and the World-Wide Revival Prayer Movement was launched, though the lusty infant had not then been named.

It was Mr. Davis who suggested the name in part. Realizing that a real work of God had been inaugurated that New Year's Day, while on his way to Peking to take up the work for which General Feng had engaged him, his thoughts were with the group of friends with whom he had so lately fellowshipped, and it was, as he wrote, while in prayer that the Spirit had whispered the words, "Revival Prayer Movement," into his listening ear. With the one desire to follow His leading, I was very favourably inclined to the name Mr. Davis had suggested, but there was something lacking, and I waited on God to see what further word He had for us. It was brought to mind that the meeting had been called to pray for revival world-wide and that the experiences through which I had passed in the missionary itinerancy of years had been the motivating principle in calling meeting. As I listened, the Spirit gently whispered into my waiting heart the words, "World-Wide Revival Prayer Movement," and all my questioning ceased.

Dr. Lowrie and the Misses Paxson and Davis were obliged to leave before the close of the meeting, when a discussion was in progress concerning the future *modus operandi*, and it was thought desirable to call a meeting for further deliberation at an early date. In the meantime, Mr. Hoste had been approached and had consented to act on the committee, while Miss Ruth Paxson had also accepted an invitation to include this new organism in her many-sided activities.

At the first meeting, ways and means for carrying on were discussed, and some thought that the card system, that is, the signing of a card, promising to give so much time daily to prayer, an effective way of uniting forces. Some were otherwise minded, myself among the minority group. It was the opinion expressed by Mr. Hoste that held this matter in abeyance for the present at least. His experience had taught that too often such a pledge led into bondage, for while under the impact of urging many thought they could keep such a resolve, frequently the result was undesirable. Later we were convinced through the Word that it was not God's way for the World-Wide Revival Prayer Movement to follow a course so many had adopted. Since our "members" have increased to thousands, we have more clearly seen the display of the wisdom which is from above. Instead of one helper, we should long ere this have been obliged to employ a force of workers to look after the tabulating and other clerical work in keeping the records and answering a huge correspondence. As it now is, the work of the Spirit functions according to His prompting and not from urging on our part.

Perhaps I should say in passing that that New Year's Day, which is the natal day of the World-Wide Revival Prayer Meeting, is observed each January 1 in prayer and fasting. The first anniversary meeting was held in the committee room of the Bible Union of China, and the notice published in the daily paper ran thus: "An all day praise and prayer service in observance of the first anniversary of the World-Wide Revival Prayer Movement will be held on New Year's Day in the Bible Union Committee Room, 4 Quinsan Gardens. Dr. Henry M. Woods will open the meeting with a short address at 11 o'clock." Each year the company of pleaders for revival increases in numbers and strength; a great company now girdles the globe.

We had determined at the first meeting to call a meeting whenever it seemed best, those who had graciously consented to serve being without exception very busy in affairs to which they were already committed. Dr. Lowrie and Mr. Hoste were, in the very nature of their calling, often absent from the city, and Dr. Robert Bryan was greatly in demand among Southern Baptists for evangelistic services. Miss Paxson had been U.S.A. Secretary of the Young Women's Christian Association in China, until Modernistic tendencies obliged her to resign, and her wide knowledge and great ability as an evangelist frequently called her away from Shanghai. When it was thought time to call the second meeting of the committee, we found that Mr. Hoste was in the far North and patiently waited his return, feeling confident that with the lion of the occasion secure, we should have no difficulty in getting a quorum. Upon his return—having had our weather-eye open—we wrote to Mr. Hoste and received word that he would meet with us. We then sent notices to others. Miss Paxson replied that she would be away at the appointed time, and that if her presence was desired at any future time she must be notified at least two weeks in advance. While we were digesting this bit of information, a *chit* was delivered in which Mr. Hoste stated with great regret that he would be obliged to attend a meeting of the National Christian Council. Matters of a very important nature having arisen, an extra meeting had been called, and he had been induced to cancel his promise to me in order to meet with that august gathering. From that time my interest in a committee waned rapidly. Other attempts were made to continue with a committee, but failed as dismally, and the "committee" died a natural death. An American wag has said, "A committee is a gathering of important people who, singly, can do nothing, but together can decide that nothing can be done."

That prince of preachers, the late C. H. Spurgeon, is credited with expressing the opinion that the ideal committee is composed of two—with one absent! And Mary Slessor, "The White Queen of Okoyong," expressed her disappointment over the results of the Edinburgh Conference of 1910 in these words, "After all, it is not committees and men's organizations from without that are to bring in the revival and send the Gospel to the heathen at home and abroad, but the living Spirit of God, working in the heart."

The World-Wide Revival Prayer Movement has gone on from strength to strength, and we trust with some degree of glory, without the *backing* of a single person. God has raised up friends—good men and true —who have been mightily used to further the great cause of revival in the body of believers and, when His time is come, will be used of the Holy Spirit to bring in the remaining members who still are not joined to the Head, Jesus Christ the Lord, but who must be added for its completion before He comes again. But we have more even than these tried and true friends; we can echo John Wesley's dying words, at the end of his long, untiring service: "The best of all is, *God* is with us."

IV

A GOLDEN LINK

AT Karuizawa, in the summer of 1919, I had
come into contact with members of the Japan
Evangelistic Band, of which Mr. A. Paget
Wilkes was the Chairman and Leader. The Rev.
Barclay Buxton founded the Band, and it was in his
summer home that the members were then located.
After the usual Missionary Conference at Karuizawa,
Mr. Wilkes gave a series of addresses on Personal
Evangelism. A regular attendant at all such gatherings, being deeply interested in all phases of Christian
work, and the main purpose of my travels being to
see such work abroad at close quarters, I listened with
intense interest to Mr. Wilkes' presentation of his subject. Very soon I discovered that here was a past master,
one who spoke "with authority, and not as the scribes."

As the lectures continued, I was made to see that
this was what the Church needed—a consciousness of
the supreme importance of the evangelistic note,
individually applied! The desire took root in my mind
that the lectures might be published in book form,
to supply a distinct need, especially that of young,
inexperienced men and women looking toward the
foreign field as their place of service for our Master.
Mr. Wilkes stressed the importance of expecting to see
immediate results. He said:

D   49

"From a long experience I have found that it is possible to lead men and women to Christ far more quickly than is supposed practicable by others. It is generally believed that a long period of instruction is necessary in non-Christian countries before we can urge men to be saved. I feel confident that this was not the way of the Master, nor of Apostolic Christianity. The natural man cannot understand the things that are spiritual; hence it is necessary that men should first 'be saved,' and then 'come to the knowledge of the truth.'"

Much more was said that focused the regenerate mind upon the value of these messages delivered by Mr. Wilkes, and which made as strong an appeal as the pointed passage quoted, and deepened the desire to see this vital matter placed in the hands of those for whom the messages seemed especially fitted. Nothing was said to the *lecturer*, but much prayer was being offered before God for the wisdom and revelation of His will, and after several weeks I was permitted to broach to Mr. Wilkes the subject that had been occupying my mind, and to make clear the concern I had felt for young people who were looking forward to the mission field as their appointed place of service.

Mr. Wilkes replied that he would welcome an opportunity to publish the lectures, but that there was no present prospect of doing it. Nothing further was said at the time, but I continued to keep the matter within the circle of prayer requests and finally, after some months—I had by this time reached China—the conviction that this desire had come forth from Him was assured, and I wrote to the lecturer, enclosing a cheque for as much as I felt I should contribute, for the specific purpose of having the book published. It was long before the desire came to fruition. The World War had had a demoralizing effect upon all commercial enterprises as well as on society in general, and it was two years or more before the first edition of *The Dynamic of Service*, as Mr. Wilkes named his book, made its appearance. The first copy reached me at Shrinagar, Kashmir, where I was spending the summer, and I lost no time in reading it from cover to cover. It deepened the conviction that here was a message of great importance to the Church. One thousand copies were immediately ordered, and Mr F. Kehl, of Calcutta, so remarkably used of God in the circulation of sound literature, undertook the work of dispatching them to strategic missionary centres in India, Burma, Kashmir and Ceylon.

Upon returning to China in the spring of 1923, the work of distribution continued, and thousands of missionaries and Christian workers were reached here and elsewhere. Letters from men and women, affiliated with different denominations, expressed the warmest appreciation for the help they had received through reading this compelling message. Dr. Egbert Smith, Executive Secretary of Foreign Missions of the Southern Presbyterian Church, while making a survey of the South American field, wrote that the book was being extensively read and its teaching absorbed. "In almost every home I visit I find a copy of *The Dynamic of Service*," he wrote in expressing his and his colleague's appreciation of this contribution to the cause of missions.

One of the hundreds of letters received will help to show how much the book was welcomed: "You gave me eighty copies of *The Dynamic of Service* for distribution through our Forward Movement Office in the U.S.A.," wrote a missionary stationed in the interior of China. "I am enclosing a clipping from our denominational paper showing the plan used to put the book in circulation among pastors, Sabbath School teachers, Gospel Team members and Personal Workers." The "plan" was that of lending, and so reaching the greatest possible number of those interested enough to apply for the book after reading the recommendation. The reception given it exceeded all expectation and, when the first edition was exhausted and the second on the press, Mr. Wilkes wrote to me, "But for your encouragement the book would never have been published."

The Dynamic of Service is undoubtedly one of the finest books ever published on Personal Evangelism. A veteran missionary after reading it several times wrote: "Thank you most cordially for your truly wonderful book, from which I have learned, at the age of seventy, more about the winning of the heathen than through any other book. No words can express how I value it." One reviewer said: "As a reliable *vade mecum* for soul-winning, this book is perhaps unexcelled. It is written by one whose Christ-honouring service in Japan makes him a professor in Evangelism of the first degree."

Mr. Wilkes himself, in the Introduction to the book, says:

"The responsibility of service is truly a Dynamic to the Soul. There are few things that move the hearts and minds of men more effectively than the sense of such responsibility. So long as the Christian's ideal is merely to live in peace and 'charity with his neighbour,' without a realization of his responsibility towards their souls, it is more than likely that he will make little progress in the way of holiness, and will moreover be ignorant of his own state before God. His spiritual bankruptcy hardly becomes apparent. As soon, however, as he begins to understand that he is 'his brother's keeper,' that no man lives unto himself, and that the humblest Christian, as in the early Church, is responsible for bringing men to Christ, then he also is made aware of his own poverty, the demand for service proves a dynamic indeed; and he bestirs himself to seek and to find, and so become fitted for the performance of his duty—the solemn yet blessed duty of saving men.

"What I have written in the following pages is in large measure the contents of a series of addresses delivered in a missionary summer resort. Repeated requests for their appearance in more permanent shape is the only apology I have for their publication. The actual purpose of their being sent forth in this form is the hope that they may be of some little help to young missionaries and candidates for the foreign field. After nearly a quarter-of-a-century of service in the mission field, I have noticed with surprise how little preparation and training seem to have been given to men and women on this most important and difficult of all themes—how to deal practically with the souls of men. In heathen lands, of course, the subject is far more difficult than at home. That great man of God, John Smith, in the early part of the last century, said, 'No man feels the value of the soul of another who has not been made sensible of the worth of his own soul. No man discerns the malignity of sin in the world who has not felt the bitterness and terror of sin in his own heart. No man is awake to the perils of the ungodly who has not trembled under the sense of personal danger. No man forms a correct estimate of the value of the Atonement who has not had the blood of Christ sprinkled on his own conscience.'"

The first chapter of the book deals with the "Dynamic of a Commission," and the intimate knowledge which the author has of his subject and the thoroughness with which he handles it may be judged from the titles of the other chapters: The Honour of the Ministry; The Condition of the Ministry; The Task—the Awakening of the Soul; the Task—the Enlightenment of the Understanding; The task—the Conversion of the Will; The Conscience Purified; The Task—the Affections Renewed.

With this background, it was most natural that my mind should turn to the author of *The Dynamic of Service* when, during the days of convalescence after weeks of serious illness several years later, the thought was given to me to ask Mr. Wilkes to come to China the next summer for special work with individual on the subject which was his speciality, at the great Conference at Kuling, the largest summer mountain resort in China. After many days of prayer I had a direct word from the Lord: "Launch out into the deep, and let down your nets for a draught"; and on the strength of this I at once wrote to Mr. Wilkes, putting before him the concern that had been laid upon my heart.

At his first answer I could, naturally speaking, entertain no further hope of the fulfilment of that which I believed God had spoken to my spirit, for his reply was a decided "No." Again I waited for further instructions. After two weeks, "I will instruct thee and teach thee," gave the added conviction that this thing was of the Lord, and so I wrote again, asking that the matter should not be dismissed as settled, but that we continue in prayer and watch in the same with thanksgiving.

Mr. Wilkes wrote from Kobe, Japan, on February 2, 1925, saying:

"Your letter under date January 31st, in reply to mine of the 25th, came to hand yesterday. Many thanks. I find it most difficult to reply to your suggestion that I come to China for Summer Conference work, and that for the following reasons: (1) We have pressing problems in our own mission which need my time, presence and attention here, (2) We have not yet heard finally whether Mr. Cuthbertson, who at present is in the States, will get back this spring, though I fear he will not. Lastly, I am not sure that my ministry would be acceptable at the Summer Conferences. As you know, the burden of my heart is what is known as the 'second blessing.' If, however, the other difficulties were removed and I had a clear call from God, I would be willing to help in any way I could."

This was certainly far from discouraging, and I continued to pray without ceasing that God might have His way in all that was involved, for in spite of the reasons Mr. Wilkes had given, including the "second blessing" belief, I could not but feel that it was God's will for him to come.

This question of the "second blessing" that Mr. Wilkes was so careful to state as his objective in preaching the unsearchable riches of Christ was somewhat of a "bone of contention" between us. I had once written to him regarding his theory of entire sanctification which we feared smacked of human "perfection," or, as some express the experience, "eradication," meaning that the redeemed person can no longer sin. This is not Scriptural, for we are told, "If we say that we have no sin, we deceive ourselves."

I did know, however, that he endeavoured to live the doctrine he and other members of the Japan Evangelistic Band held as a cardinal preparation for effective service and, having seen the Band in action and knowing of the truly wonderful results achieved by some of its members in soul saving and sanctified living, we were not disposed to make an issue of the declaration contained in this letter. And the marvellous way the Holy Spirit was to use Mr. Wilkes in the Shanghai meetings proved that God is greater than the difference of opinion held by many good and faithful servants of His, who do not see eye to eye on all the doctrinal constructions placed on certain portions of His Divine Word.

We could go on with Mr. Wilkes this far, that, as expressed by the late Dr. R. A. Torrey:

"A man may be regenerated by the Holy Spirit and still not be baptized with the Holy Spirit. In regeneration there is an impartation of life, and the one who receives it is saved; in the baptism with the Holy Spirit there is an impartation of power, and the one who receives it is fitted for service. The doctrine of the baptism with the Holy Spirit has been so allowed to drop out of sight and the Church has so little expectancy along this line for its young children that a large portion of the churches are in the position of the churches at Ephesus and Samaria, where someone has to come and call the mass of believers to their privilege in the risen Christ and claim it for themselves. Which statement exactly coincides with our interpretation of the believers' legitimate rights in Christ Jesus."

Thousands have experienced the "second blessing" described by Dr. Torrey. As a bit of personal experience, I may say that while a young girl, the Spirit convicted me of sin and the need of a Saviour, and I was converted. Then a few years later came the further blessing of separation, or sanctification—a quiet work of the Holy Spirit as I sat alone in a room with a bit of needlework in my hands, my thoughts occupied with the words, "I beseech you therefore by the mercies of God, that ye present your bodies a living sacrifice, holy, acceptable unto God, which is your reasonable service. And be not conformed to this world; but be ye transformed by the renewing of your mind, that ye may prove what is that good, and acceptable, and perfect will of God." My reasoning—though not in the exact words—was parallel with Hebrews 12: 9: "Furthermore we have had fathers of our flesh which corrected us, and we gave them reverence (or obedience) : shall we not much rather be in subjection unto the Father of spirits and live?"

Strangely enough, the arresting words that caused me to pause and consider well the meaning of these verses in Romans 12: 1, 2 were "your reasonable service," and He has been transforming ever since. It is the altar that sanctifies the gift; the gift in itself is of no worth.

The members of the Japan Evangelistic Band are not alone in embracing the doctrine of entire sanctification, or the second blessing, or, again, as some express it, eradication, though this last name always disturbed Mr. Wilkes exceedingly, as, "It is not a Scriptural term," he would say. Hundreds of the godliest men and women, whose lives are "living epistles" known and read of all with whom they come into contact, hold the same views as the friends we have mentioned. So long as the great cardinal doctrines of the Bible are adhered to—the Virgin Birth of our Lord, the Sacrifice on the Cross of Calvary as a propitiation for sins, "and not for ours only, but also for the sins of the whole world," the resurrection of the Saviour's body from the tomb—we join hands with all who believe these things which are revealed to the soul by the Holy Spirit.

Later my heart was gladdened by news from Mr. Wilkes contained in a letter dated April 3 :

"Thanks for your kind letter of March 25th. I have now received a cable from Mr. Cuthbertson saying that he will be returning in May. So that I think I may say that my wife and I will be very pleased to accept your kind invitation to visit China. *The Empress of Canada* leaves Kobe on the 23rd or 24th of June, arriving at Shanghai on the 26th. We shall hope to come by this boat."

Their views widely divergent on a matter of mission policy, these brethren, like their predecessors Paul and Barnabas, had contended so sharply that they departed asunder one from the other, Mr. Cuthbertson going to the States and Mr. Wilkes remaining in Japan to settle if possible the trouble that was rending the Band.

On April 23 Mrs. Wilkes wrote:

"As things really seem to be shaping themselves with regard to our visit to China, before meeting you I feel I must write and thank you so much for including me specially, as I am not a 'Speaker' nor a 'Platform Lady' *at all*. But I do feel it will relieve you all to think my husband has someone with him who can see after him! And I shall enjoy coming immensely. I felt all along that it was in God's plan for him to go, a stepping-stone for wider service. We are much in prayer about this visit, trusting that God will keep us in His will every step of the way."

But a great deal had happened in Shanghai before their arrival and, indeed, before Mr. Wilkes' next letter, of June 4, arrived:

"News in the Japanese papers concerning the state of things in China in general and Shanghai in particular make me wonder if your summer programme will proceed as planned. I am holding myself in readiness to sail or cancel sailing, as you shall direct. If at the last moment you advise against our coming, you will wire us in time, won't you? It may be, of course, that our papers have exaggerated the situation."

It would have been difficult to exaggerate the situation, as will be seen, and after the meetings were well under way and the violent disturbances still continued, Mr. Wilkes reminded me that but for my interest in the Japan Evangelistic Band they would not have been there. And despite untoward circumstances, the result of the meetings was, as Mrs. Wilkes had written, "a stepping-stone" to a wider ministry for her husband who, after leaving Japan, never returned, several attempts being frustrated. This wider service came through extensive travels in evangelistic work, first to South Africa and then in other parts of the world. Again it was "the woman thou gavest me" who led the way, though, unlike our Mother Eve, this was in the right direction.

V

REVIVAL OR RIOT

IT has been said of the great Apostle to the Gentiles, Saint Paul, that during the whole of his career he experienced either a Revival or a Riot continuously. His personal record of the events which filled and overflowed his whole existence as a follower of the Lord Jesus Christ, from the moment of that momentous meeting on the Damascus Road, bears out the truth of this statement. Take one instance only, when with Silas he was apprehended for the preaching of the Gospel of Jesus Christ committed to him, and after being beaten with many stripes, their feet held in stocks, thrust into the inner prison, they sang songs —songs of victory that they were accounted worthy to suffer for His sake. Then, lo, the doors of the prison were opened by an unseen hand, and the cruel jailor with all his house was converted! Truly, a revival, for which praise could be ascribed only to God the Holy Spirit.

The entire book of The Acts is a record of the working of the Holy Spirit through "earthen vessels, that the excellency of the power might be of God and not of man." In chapter 4: 33 we read: "And with great power gave the apostles witness to the resurrection of the Lord Jesus: and great grace was upon them all," the "all" being those who had believed in the Lord

Jesus and had experienced the baptism of the Holy Spirit at Pentecost. Is not the main reason for the absence of the evident working of God in this day and generation accounted for on the ground of ignoring the Holy Spirit? The Word of God is not spoken with the boldness that results in supernatural testimony to the fulness of the Third Person of the Trinity. A minister and evangelist has said that "Died of Respectability" is the epitaph that should be placed on the bulletin boards of many of our churches. Be that as it may, it is a recognized fact that the Church is suffering from a prolonged attack of pernicious anæmia, and the only thing that can infuse new life and prolong her usefulness is blood transfusion from Him who died on Calvary's cross, that we might have life and have it more abundantly.

It was the riot in the great port city of Shanghai that spring of 1925 that led to the Revival, the effect of which is felt to this day and will continue for many days to come. We do not think we are claiming too much to say its influence has spread a revival spirit throughout the world. We will attempt to describe the conditions which brought about this unexpected blessing, though much prayer had been made for many months preceding.

A group of insurgent students, gathered in a room for the purpose of fomenting trouble, were found by the police and taken to the station. In the fracas, shots were fired, and unfortunately one of the ringleaders was hit in the back with a bullet. Evidence given on behalf of the Shanghai police by a member of the China Inland Mission staff, who was an eye-

witness to the disturbance, created a widespread
impression among the Chinese that these good people
had turned to be enemies, and this propaganda had
gone throughout China. Anti-foreign feeling became
rampant, for the telegraph quickly carried news of
the trouble that had arisen to all parts of the great
land. This was the determining factor in the decisions
of the British Consul and of the Stewart Evangelistic
Committee, to recall our invitations to Messrs. Wilkes
and Howden, of which I must later speak. Small
wonder that Mr. Howden expressed the possibility of
a recurrence of the awful days of the Boxer Uprising.

The city of Shanghai before long was in a state of
siege. British and Americans were treated alike; a
boycott soon developed and only with difficulty could
sufficient food be secured. No one who lived in China
during those troublous times will ever forget the
alarming situation. Dixwell Road, where our house
was located, in the Japanese Concession, is a good two
miles from the business district. Only when necessary
did we venture out. We had no automobile. The
money that we had been sorely tempted to invest in
one had gone into rebates on copies of the *Encyclopedia*,
thereby making available many thousands of copies
to poor evangelists and pastors, including nearly a
thousand copies to the China Inland Mission, so that
we had no reason to regret the renunciation of an
automobile, but rather rejoiced in it. The usual means
of travel, the rickshaw, was unsafe, and the tram-car,
our next recourse, was almost as dangerous, for hardly
a car had whole windows. Miscreants, hiding in
alleyways along the tram route, would hurl stones,

endangering the lives of the occupants, so that very few dared risk riding in the trams.

On one occasion when compelled to go to Nanking Road, the shopping section, I chose the tram as being safer and less exposed to possible violence than the rickshaw. One other occupant, a gentleman, had squeezed into the far corner from the place which I had chosen, to get as far out of sight as was possible; suddenly I saw him drop forward face downward on the floor. But before he reached this position of safety a huge stone came hurtling through the window scattering broken glass in every direction. Fortunately, I was far enough removed to escape injury, nor did the intended victim sustain real hurt, thanks to an over-ruling Providence.

On another occasion, thinking that the cook, a Chinese, would be able to get supplies denied us, we sent him to market with a five-dollar bill and instructions as to his purchases. It is the custom in China for the cook to do the marketing and it is understood that he will make a profit called "squeeze"; that is, he buys supplies for a certain amount and sells to the house-holder at an advance. Any one trying to alter this law, as fixed as that of the Medes and Persians, would soon find himself without servants. After a reasonable length of time, the cook returned white (?) and trembling, with an *empty basket*. This was the story he told: Having bought the meat and vegetables, he set out upon the return trip; when about halfway home he was held up by Chinese soldiers and, at the point of a bayonet, was relieved of his purchases. Trying to calm him, I suggested that he try again, as the stock of food was exceedingly low. Shaking his head, he said, "Me no savvy. Soldiers very fierce!" and our persuasions failed.

Agitators were sent throughout the streets of Shanghai to induce servants of foreigners to leave their places of employment. On one occasion we were attracted to a back window by hearing sounds that boded no good. There stood a man pounding on the gate and demanding entrance. Our faithful cook, very much upset, still refused to open the gate. After a prolonged and utterly futile attempt to accomplish his purpose, the trouble-maker moved on. We were among the comparatively few Europeans who did not lose their servants. All three of ours stayed "by the stuff."

Of course, missionaries were included in the general feeling against foreigners; and the cloud of suspicion slowly obscured the love and confidence of the Chinese for those who for half-a-century or more had laboured in season and out of season for their highest good. As an indication of the spirit which prevailed, this incident will suffice. At one of the interior stations of a denominational mission, the Boys' School had just had the closing exercises, when the trouble broke out. Each lad had been presented with a New Testament, for all had confessed their faith in the foreign doctrine. As soon as the news of the riot in Shanghai reached this point—the day after the closing exercises and before the boys had left the school—they came in a body to the Principal, bringing the Testaments with them, and standing before him they tore the pages into fragments. The intense feeling that

E

existed everywhere cannot be exaggerated, and it was at such a time as this that our faithful God raised up a standard against the enemy who had indeed come in like a flood.

Though the trouble had not abated but rather grown worse, there had been no change in the plan to have Mr. Wilkes come to China, though the place for the meetings had been changed from necessity. The trouble was now so widespread, the temper of the people so brittle and unreliable, that all thought of conducting the regular Conferences at Kuling had been abandoned, and with the co-operation of the Milton Stewart Evangelistic Committee it had been arranged to have meetings in Shanghai. Arrangements were as nearly perfected as was possible when, on the morning of June 19, I received a cable reading, "Shall we postpone sailing until more settled?" signed "Wilkes." I was fairly stunned at the turn of events. Immediately I set myself to inquire further as to the Lord's will, and after a few minutes had the definite impression that I should cable that there was no alteration in the plans. How little I knew what was going on at that very moment in the Committee Room of the Stewart Evangelistic Committee!

On Wednesday, June 17, I had received the following communication from the Rev. Elwood G. Tewksbury, chairman of that Committee, with whom I had frequently conferred regarding possibilities of the meetings:

"To continue our conversation of yesterday morning, would say that at the meeting of the China Conference Committee, I spoke of your thought of having evangelistic meetings in Shanghai led by Messrs. Paget Wilkes and Rev. J. Russell Howden.

"The Committee first considered whether the first Kuling Bible Study Conference should be postponed or not, and voted that it would be unwise under present circumstances to do otherwise than postpone it.

"They then asked Mr. Longdon to see the friends at the C.I.M. (China Inland Mission) and get their advice, not only with regard to calling the conference, but also to suggest that Mr. Howden do so. There we saw Messrs. Gibbs and Stark and the Misses Tippett and Margaret King. They felt that the conference should be called off, and heartily agreed that a series of evangelistic meetings held in Shanghai for the foreigners for the deepening of the spiritual life, personal work, etc., would be very desirable.

"I am therefore instructed to so inform you, to tell you that we are quite willing to ask Mr. Howden to take part in the campaign, if you will do the same with regard to Mr. Wilkes. Praying with you that God may greatly bless both the plans and the campaign, if it is decided upon, and hoping that you may have your suggestion ready for me to pass on to the Committee which hopes to meet again on Friday."

And now Friday, the 19th, had arrived, the day of the meeting and the day of Mr. Wilkes' cable. The die was to be cast, and I now have reason to believe that at the very hour I passed by the room where the Committee was to meet, on my way to the telegraph office, deliberations were going on which led to the withdrawal of the support I had counted upon.

The worst was yet to come, but it furnished a grand opportunity to prove that, "All things work together for good to them that love God, to them who are the called according to his purpose" (Rom. 8:28). How well we were to know this, though through much tribulation! The Great Northern Telegraph Company's office was situated a good three miles from where we lived, and the only means of reaching it was by rickshaw. However, some of the men who draw these vehicles are amazingly strong and swift. So, beginning preparations, praying as I did so and turning over in mind the best way to convey the message so that there would be no possibility of a double interpretation, earnestly asking to be plainly guided, suddenly there flashed into my mind the one word "Come," and I *knew* that this was His own answer.

We had left the house with the intention of stopping to see Mr. Tewksbury. His office, as representative of the Sunday School Union, was just around the corner on Quinsan Road which we must pass as we "drove" down Woosing Road. As we approached the street we began to have questionings as to whether we should see him then or later. The conflict of thought became so sharp that, in the intensity of desire to *know what He would have us do*, I closed my eyes for what seemed only a second; but the fleet-footed "steed" had carried me past the corner when I again looked around, so I could but conclude that the news was to wait for a more convenient season.

Having sent off the cable, I had perfect rest of spirit, no questions intruding as to what the friends would think of my action. The next day, Saturday, Dr. Lowrie, a very important member of the Stewart Committee, called. I had gone out for a little walk and so missed seeing him. Dr. Woods was in bed with summer grippe, and thus we had no means of knowing for what purpose he had called.

On Sunday, the 21st, about noon, the boy came up to say that "Two Piece downstairs, Miss Paxson one." At once we felt that this visit had something to do with the proposed meetings, and that this thought was right we soon discovered. Miss Paxson had come, as representative of the Stewart Evangelistic Committee, to inform me that after prolonged deliberations it had been determined to refer the matter of the advisability of holding public meetings under the existing difficult conditions to the British Consul. That gentleman, after considering the risk as far as was possible, strongly advised against any attempt along these lines. The determining factor in his decision I have referred to. Miss Paxson then suggested that I cable Mr. Wilkes, as they had planned to cable Dr. Howden, who was to arrive at Kobe the following Wednesday, and cancel the invitation; she also asked that I suggest that Mr. Wilkes accompany Dr. Howden on a forced evangelistic tour of Japan.

To me this was not feasible for the very good reason that, as I told Miss Paxson, the date was now so late that arrangements for speakers at the different conventions had been made, though I said I would give the names of friends who might be called upon for such a service as they wished Mr. Wilkes to take. I gave the name of Dr. Harry Meyers who lived at Kobe and who would be willing, I was inclined to believe, to help in the way desired, though I knew nothing of plans he might already have made.

At the time I said nothing about the cable to Mr. Wilkes. As a matter of fact, wholly unprepared for the information just received, my mind could only grapple with the present exigency. During the evening of that same Sunday, Dr. Lowrie called again, and in his gentle way tried to persuade me to abandon all thoughts of the meetings planned, suggesting, as Miss Paxson had done, that a cable be sent to Mr. Wilkes calling off his engagement. During the intervening hours my mind had become adjusted to the new developments, and I told Dr. Lowrie that it was now too late to alter the plans, as two days before I had cabled Mr. Wilkes to come, hastening, as I saw the shock this news produced, to add that he and his colleagues were in no wise involved. "I suppose nothing more can be done," he then said, and I admitted that it would seem so, as the matter was as definitely settled as circumstances permitted, and that I felt assured of the sympathy and prayerful co-operation of the Stewart Committee, to which he most cordially assented.

Now, please observe the way the *Lord* led. At the very hour when the Spirit was exercising my mind about stopping to see Mr. Tewksbury, the committee was in session considering the momentous question of whether the meetings were "to be or not to be." To have acted contrary to the decision would have alienated their support, or quite probably caused the abandonment of the meetings altogether.

In his book, *My Mission to China*, the Rev. J. Russell Howden tells something of the perturbation of spirit he and his wife felt when, upon reaching Kobe, they found the cable requesting that they stay in Japan and not venture on to China. As they waited upon God, however, the conviction grew that having been called to *China*, to *China* they must go! He writes:

"As soon as the decision had been reached, our minds were at ease about the matter. It seemed to us just then in the light of all the information we could gather that God's dear people in China might already be facing a recurrence of the Boxer Uprising. However, we arrived at our decision and sent off our cable in reply. And half-an-hour after, we were astonished and delighted to see Mr. and Mrs. Paget Wilkes coming aboard, bound themselves for Shanghai to take a series of meetings for which some friends there had asked, in view of the great crisis. Here was a swift confirmation given just when it meant so much to us. It was just like God, who knows His creatures' weakness, to do a thing like that. And Eliezer's thankful acknowledgment came unbidden to one's memory, 'I being in the way the Lord led me.' "

I need not add that these same words apply to the personal experiences related. This experience of cabling to Mr. Wilkes, coming as it did even before the meetings started, caused great watchfulness as well as prayerfulness.

The meetings started June 28 and continued until the first of September. No wonder it was of great importance to God's cause that Mr. Howden came to Shanghai. For it was he whom the Lord mightily used in the last three meetings, addressing crowds that filled the Union Church to suffocation during the last days of the Revival. As Mr. Leland Wang wrote me later,

"God certainly has caughed you to triumph," for those last meetings in the variety of nationalities represented resembled Pentecost—British, Americans, Japanese, Chinese, Portuguese, French, and the many others which only New York, London or Shanghai could furnish.

VI

THE SHANGHAI REVIVAL

THE day of arrival had come, and Mr. and Mrs. Wilkes and the Rev. and Mrs. Howden were due in Shanghai in the course of Friday, June 26, at four o'clock in the afternoon. Being assured that this was so, we arranged for a reception the following day, Saturday, but with conditions so uncertain the invitations were taken with us when we went to meet the boat, but not mailed until we had seen the friends on Chinese soil. A goodly company greeted them, for all having an invitation had braved the uncertainty of the surcharged atmosphere, though it was not until late that Misses Paxson and Davis appeared, explaining their non-appearance at an earlier hour by saying that the invitation posted the previous afternoon had not reached their home in Frenchtown until three o'clock, when they immediately set out for our home to meet the distinguished friends from abroad. It was a happy and profitable time, a time for explanations and reaffirmations of co-operation. We were charmed with our visitors, and especially impressed with Dr. Howden's gracious and humble personality.

During the interval between the riot on May 30 and the time of the expected arrival of Mr. Wilkes and Dr. Howden, one verse of Scripture had echoed over and over in my mind, "Do as occasion serve thee, for

God is with thee." The "occasion" proved to be the evacuation of missionary stations and consequent revival of hundreds in Shanghai. The meetings for missionaries continued for three full weeks and during this period, to our utter astonishment, a number of the higher class Chinese, all young people, had been in daily attendance. A young Chinese woman—member of the Christian and Missionary Alliance—had felt a special concern for her own people to share more fully in the blessing so manifestly of the Spirit, and this possibility for carrying on had been causing considerable exercise of spirit among the leaders.

The meetings began first in a small room formerly used for the Missionary Prayer Meeting and then the Union Church was opened to us.

In the first little pamphlet issued, giving a short record of His working, which was kept in a notebook for personal use, without any thought of a wider ministry, I find this:

"We had not definitely determined how long the Conference should last (we had not then sensed that God was doing a marvellous work in reviving), and it was at the end of the ten days which we tentatively had set for its duration that Miss Jennie Hughes, colleague of Dr. Mary Stone, of Bethel, came to me with the question of what to do about the tram service. She said, 'The contract expires to-day, and if we do not notify the tram company before night we shall not have conveyances for the delegates to-morrow. Shall the Conference go on another week?'"

Some over-zealous person had published abroad the news that the Conference would close this very day,

July 30. We felt "an enemy hath done this," for there was no release in spirit, and we knew not how much longer the Spirit would carry on the meetings. We replied, "Take the trams for another ten days," and then when she had gone, wondered if there would be any one to use those trams. By faith we went forward, step by step. The contract was renewed, and the entertainment at Bethel was extended for another ten days. On another occasion quite as critical, the Angel of the Lord guided Miss Martha Jewell, who was not a usual attendant at the daily prayer meetings, to come with a message of such spiritual stimulus that victory was brought out of seeming defeat. The words given her from the Lord were: "Cast not away therefore your confidence, which hath great recompence of reward."

A splendid account of the meetings was given in the *North China Daily News*, headed "Many Attending Revival Series. Chinese and Foreigners Join in Movement:"

"In connection with the series of revival meetings which have been attended by hundreds of Chinese and foreigners in the Union Church during the past two months, many have inquired as to the origin of this spiritual movement. This religious awakening originated in the formation of a prayer band, known as 'The World-Wide Revival Prayer Movement,' in the home of Dr. and Mrs. Henry M. Woods, of the Southern Presbyterian Mission, 715 Dixwell Road, when a small group of Christian workers met to pray for revival in January (1924). Since that time many in India, England and America, as well as hundreds in various parts of China, have learned of this Revival Prayer

Movement and have joined in prayer for world-wide revival.

"While the special meetings have been in progress daily in the Union Church, groups of missionaries have been gathering for prayer on behalf of these meetings in Kuling, Peitaiho, Kikungshan, Mohkanshan and other places in China, several days having been set apart for fasting and prayer. Cablegrams have also been received from India and America by Mrs. Woods, telling of similar prayer meetings there.

"Each day while Mr. Paget Wilkes or others were preaching in Union Church, a group of men were assembled for prayer in one of the rooms in the Church Hall, under the leadership of Dr. Woods, and a group of ladies were also meeting for prayer in another room, led by Mrs. Woods. It has been the earnest desire of all who have been meeting daily for prayer that genuine spiritual revival might begin here in Shanghai at this time of political unrest, which would spread throughout the whole of China and to the ends of the world.

"The address by the Rev. J. Russell Howden, D.D., of London, was much appreciated by the large audience of Chinese and foreigners; this was the first of the series of addresses which Dr. Howden is to deliver each afternoon at 5:15 P.M."

We do not know to this day who was responsible for the press notices of the meetings, not a line was sent by us personally.

VII

STRENGTHENING THE STAKES

THE great interest resulting from the distribution of *The Dynamic of Service* had made the missionaries keenly expectant of Mr. Wilkes' visit to China, and no further effort was needed to advertise the meetings. Through an over-ruling Providence, the disturbances literally drove the missionaries in to Shanghai for protection, upon the necessity of the evacuation of their respective stations, and a far larger number were thereby reached than would have otherwise been possible, a most colourful group, denominationally speaking. A leading of more than ordinary import came when, as the missionary meetings were drawing to a close, the Chinese themselves asked for a continuance of the work. We were indeed in a tight corner, for Mr. Wilkes had never spoken by interpretation, and so far as we could see, there was no one available for this important work; but impossibilities were not the exceptions but rather the order of every day.

It was after a morning prayer meeting at our home that the question of an interpreter for the speaker to the Chinese came up for serious consideration. We knelt in a little circle to pray for guidance, and while on our knees the name of Evangelist Leland Wang was brought to mind. As we rose from this time of intensive waiting upon God, Mr. Wang's name was suggested. All those present who knew him agreed that he would be the best interpreter possible; but where could he be found? That was the question. No one there knew of his whereabouts. The last heard of him was that he was conducting meetings in Shantung Province; there was nothing more definite than that to go upon. This province has nearly 60,000 square miles and a population of 40,000,000 people. To look for a man in this vast area would be less likely of results than to look for a needle in a haystack. However, prayer had been made and we trusted HIM who never fails the believing heart.

Our next concern was for someone who could deliver a message with an interpreter, as the medium to get the full value to the people. The Rev. J. B. Thornton, an American at this time associated with the Japan Evangelistic Band, a colleague of Mr. Wilkes, was thought of to fill this pressing need. Though a missionary of long standing in Japan, Mr. Thornton always used an interpreter, never having acquired the language of the country. On July 13, a very "lucky day" for those being used in the revival meetings, the friends met again for the purpose of praying for a revelation of HIS will. It was at this time we determined to approach Mr. Thornton regarding the possibility of securing his help. Mr. Wilkes rather discouraged sending a cable, which seemed the quickest and best way of finding whether he were available, and he strongly urged writing a letter setting forth the details, thinking that this might make a stronger appeal. The letter was written and the cable sent, so both of us had liberty in the matter.

On the morning of the 14th, after a wakeful night of prayer, it was impressed upon my mind to acquaint Dr. Dora Yu, a beloved Chinese evangelist and Bible teacher, with the work which promised such far-reaching results. Dr. Yu had been conducting a Bible Conference on the premises of the Bible Study and Prayer House, which was her home as well as a Training School for Chinese girls and women. Knowing that she would be free, we were anxious to enlist her cooperation. We suggested, while taking breakfast, that we drive out to Kiangwan, where the School was located, and that we should go before the prayer meeting at ten o'clock. All with one accord objected to the hour, and the feeling was expressed that after the meeting would be a better time. To escape from the mild but insistent babel of voices, we went to the kitchen and told the cook to go to the nearest garage and secure a "Ford." He immediately set off, and we waited with not too tranquil a mind for his return. After what seemed hours, he came and, with a broad smile, informed me that he was unable to get a Ford; he had gone to a place farther away, and beamingly said, "No could get small car, Missi; got big one." My heart sank, for a bigger car meant a bigger price. However, there was nothing to do but set off, as time was slipping away, and the prayer meeting at ten o'clock was of first importance (so we thought at the time). We drove the five miles as rapidly as possible. On arriving we were met with the astonishing news that Mr. Leland Wang was there! Miss Yu explained that he had arrived in Shanghai from Shantung the night before, and had come out to see her about conducting some meetings at

Foochow, his home town. "Mr. Wang has been here about two minutes, and we were just going to the S.S. Office to purchase our tickets for Foochow." Who would dare to interfere with God's time-piece? Had we waited until eleven o'clock we should have been too late, and all might have been lost. Despite all opposition and the fear of being considered self-opinionated it pays to listen; and listening we shall hear what HE will say—then follow HIS leading.

Our mission having been accomplished with the "exceeding abundantly" added, we prepared to return in order to meet the friends who would come for prayer at ten o'clock. Dr. Yu lingered to make some slight change in her dress, while the rest of us stood around the car waiting for her appearance. From an open window her voice reached us with the question, whether there would be room for the Bible Woman who was exceedingly eager to go to the prayer meeting. The front seat was to be occupied by the chauffeur, Messrs. Wilkes and Wang, and the three ladies needed all the space provided by the rear seat. We looked at one another, and then as if by common consent looked at the driver. This stolid individual said nothing, but simply reached into the car and brought out a camp-stool, the space between the back and front seats of the *larger* car provided room, and shortly we were all, the Bible Woman included, happily bound for Shanghai.

I am just simple enough to believe that GOD had taken into account this humble servant of His, when He allowed the disappointment about the Ford. Some days later, after the prayer meetings which were conducted each day during the service in the church, Dr.

DR. DORA YÜ WITH A SUMMER CONFERENCE GROUP

The Bible Study and Prayer House is now the property of the Bible Seminary for Women.
Miss Ruth Brittan is Principal.

Yu came and, taking my hand, led me to a group of Chinese women who were on their faces in the court-yard of the church, pouring out their hearts to God and oblivious of all around. The tears rained down her face, and theirs also were bathed in tears. And lo, this Bible Women led all the rest! PRAYER was the secret of success of the Shanghai Revival, making it a vital, enduring testimony to the power of the Holy Spirit in this twentieth century.

The very next day, July 15, came a cable from Mr. Thornton, "Can come, but Karuizawa, August 12." Now we began to see God's hand very plainly. Strengthened and encouraged by what we had wit-nessed of HIS working, we pressed forward. July 18 was spent in prayer, fasting and praise. This meeting, as we recall, inaugurated an advance. The trustees of Union Church, a church with a British constituency, had very graciously consented to allow meetings to be held in this sacred edifice; never before had a Chinese worshipped there. Upon the arrival of Mr. Thornton the meetings took on new life and vigour. Mr. Wilkes had been under great pressure in his own work, of which he was chairman, and came to Shanghai very greatly depleted physically. Mrs. Wilkes was well aware of his condition and, though not well herself, was her husband's "right hand." Mr. Thornton was entertained in the hospitable home of Rev. John Woodberry, of the Christian and Missionary Alliance, whose household comprised his two daughters, Misses Ethel and Ora, and his son Earl and wife, the latter having recently come from the States, and this gifted musician was a great help as our organist. The entire

F

family were deeply interested in the meetings. Miss Ora also contributed to the music with her violin. The whole family were in attendance at almost every meeting, until the father and two daughters left for Mokanshan where they had a summer cottage.

Mr. Thornton told us that the letter written by Mr. Wilkes, when we were in need of someone to carry on who was accustomed to speak through an interpreter, had never reached him. Had we been dissuaded from the purpose to send him the cable message, he would still have been ignorant of the pressing need. How pressing none of us realized until, soon after Mr. Thornton's arrival, Mr. Wilkes, having had such hard work before coming, was obliged to rest a week. This we did not learn about until two years later when Mr. and Mrs. Braithwaite of Tokyo paid us a visit and told us of Mr. Wilkes' nervous exhaustion from a long period of difficulties in his own mission. Then we understood why he needed the week of rest during the Shanghai meetings, needed to cease all activity and just rest.

The most cordial co-operation existed among all the workers in Shanghai and elsewhere. After the winds of adversity had died down somewhat, some of the more intrepid ventured to the different hill stations, Kuling, Mokanshan and Peitaiho. To these friends we sent S O S messages. The letter from Miss Paxson, from Peitaiho Beach, North China, throws light upon the relationship which the Holy Spirit maintained in the members of His Body during those many weeks of spiritual combat:

"Your telegram to Mr. Longdon reached us Saturday night, and we made the meetings in Shanghai the theme of our early Sunday morning prayer meeting, and I am sure a number also fasted during the day. We continue to pray for the meetings in Shanghai and rejoice in all that God has accomplished and will accomplish during these meetings.

"Dr. Howden is better and able to take his work this week, in fact he is speaking twice a day. He will continue through the mornings of next week, and I rather think now that we will close the Conference a week from this Friday, instead of the following Monday. With this in view, it would probably be a long hard trip to take for just two or three days at the Conference here at Peitaiho, but as Miss Davis and I have prayed about the Tsingtao Conference, we have been led to ask you if it would be possible for Mr. Wilkes, if his health permits, to go to that conference, the dates for which are from August 22nd through the 31st. It does not seem wise for Dr. Howden in his present condition of health to go there, and Dr. Mack is very eager to take an earlier boat home on account of pressing duties in his Seminary work. Besides all this, I believe that one who has been accustomed to working in the Orient, and especially one whom God has so manifestly used among the Chinese in Shanghai, would be better for this work in the Chinese Conference in this present situation. . . .

"Please express our deepest sympathy to Mr. Wilkes in his illness, and tell him that many people here at Peitaiho are praying for him. I hope both you and Dr. Woods have kept well during these weeks when you have been under heavy strain."

With the return to Japan of Mr. and Mrs. Wilkes on August 10, Mr. Thornton having preceded them by two weeks, the Bethel Mission friends now withdrew their much appreciated and valuable support. Dr. Mary Stone, the noted Chinese physician, who with her beloved friend and co-worker, Miss Jennie Hughes, had in 1920 founded the Bethel Mission in Shanghai, attended the meetings, and there caught the vision which resulted in the formation of "The Bethel Bands," which from that day to this have been used of the Holy Spirit to spread revival interest, not only in China but also in the Philippine Islands and abroad. Evangelist Leland Wang had to leave also; we were therefore obliged to depend upon the like-minded local friends for speakers, which meant casting ourselves and our cares upon Him indeed and in truth, and moment by moment.

"Therefore I will look unto the Lord; I will wait for the God of my salvation: my God will hear me."

As chairman of the now non-existent Committee of the World-Wide Revival Prayer Movement and the prime mover in starting the meetings, the responsibility of securing speakers fell to my lot. The meetings of the week directly followed the departure of the friends mentioned were addressed by different Shanghai pastors. Pastor Kaung, one of the leading pastors, spoke on Monday, and then gave notice that he would not be available for further service. The following day God gave me a message, about seven hundred persons were present, and all were greatly surprised at the close to see a British lady accompanied by a Chinese woman rapidly make their way to the front of the church where I stood. Miss Abercrombie, Superintendent of "The Door of Hope," soon explained that the woman

with her desired to give a testimony, and to this request
we gladly assented. With a radiant face she faced the
large audience among whom there were a goodly number of Europeans, and told of what God had done for
her within the past few days.

She had lived in Shanghai all her life, yet had never
heard the Gospel. In some way (we know that it was
by the Spirit), she was guided to the meetings during
the previous week. Her heart was touched. She realised
herself a sinner and was saved by God's grace. She
was the first concubine of a man of considerable means.
His wife had been entirely separated from him, though
as we understand it, living under the same roof. This
"precious wife" had borne him eight children, four of
whom are still living. She returned to her home after
hearing the "Good News," and, while her heart was
filled with "joy in the Lord," a deep conviction of
the sinfulness of her life did much to mar this joy.
Finally, on the morning of August 11, the Spirit of
Truth said to her, "Go to-day to the Door of Hope.
If you don't go to-day, you will be lost." The urging
was so strong that, without delay, she presented herself
at "The Door of Hope" and told Miss Abercrombie
the Superintendent, her story.

Listening sympathetically as always, and seeking the
guidance of the Spirit, realizing that eternal life was
at stake, Miss Abercrombie, at the conclusion of the
woman's story, said, "We must send for your husband." He came, and this "precious wife" told him
exactly the state of her mind. He said, "I have known
you were different for several days." "Yes," she said,
"from the day I first heard the Gospel. Now I feel

that God is calling me to serve Him." Freely their tears flowed; he wept and she wept, and at the conclusion of the interview, voluntarily, he offered to give her the two youngest children and, with them, she went out from his home, not accepting one penny for the support of herself and children. She went to friends to prepare for the work of an evangelist.

One of God's gracious provisions for speakers came through members of the Council of the Northern Presbyterian Church, which met in Shanghai during the weeks of the continuation of the Conference for the Chinese. As an illustration of how wonderfully we were guided in the matter of procuring an acceptable speaker, one afternoon during the service I felt impelled to go round to the China Inland Mission Compound. Because of the feeling engendered by the testimony of one of the members of this mission at the time of the riot in May, we had not called upon these friends, but now we felt the impression strong to go there, though we did not then expect to secure a speaker, for much needed prayer-help. Slipping quietly away, we called a rickshaw and soon reached the Compound. Almost the first persons we saw were the Rev. and Mrs. Alexander Saunders, members from the interior, who had but just arrived. Mrs. Saunders, in a letter recently received, calls to remembrance that Spirit-guided interview. "I have," she wrote, "been remembering this morning the time of the meetings in Shanghai which brought forth your book, *The Half Can Never Be Told*. We were staying in Shanghai and, I think, spending the afternoon with the dear Broomhalls (he is now with the Lord), and you came in and asked Mr. Saunders to have a time of prayer, and we all joined in."

Nor was this all of the fellowship that the leading of the Spirit furnished, for when I somewhat timidly mentioned the need of a speaker the next day, I was delightedly surprised to find that Mr. Saunders would gladly accept the appointment, Mrs. Saunders seconding the motion with the utmost cordiality. Here indeed was a living link with the dread past—the Boxer Uprising of 1900. The Saunders family had been among the greatest sufferers at that time, hounded from one hiding-place to another, driven on foot over almost impassable roads, as they wrote:

"Tramping through heavy mud sometimes over our ankles, but we praised God for it and for the dark, cloudy flight. We were hunted and driven along the roads from village to village by howling mobs; we were stoned, clubbed, thrown to the ground and belaboured with sticks, bricks or anything else they could lay their hands on; we were spit upon, buffeted and subjected to many indignities, but we proved God's grace sufficient to bear all unmurmuringly for Jesus' sake. . . .

"Bareheaded and under a summer sun, barefooted and seven hundred miles from our destination, penniless and face-to-face with starvation, almost without clothes (the Boxers had stripped them of all but a thin shirt each) and weary with the long night's tramp, what could we do? Had God forsaken us? Would not the heathen say, 'Where is now their God?' Ah, yes, there were times when such questions did arise and when we were surrounded by doubts and fears. We truly passed through deep waters, but all praise be to His glorious Name, they did not overflow us."

Their two little daughters, Isabel and Jessie, were a sacrifice to the god of vengeance, for truly Satanic forces were let loose and the interior missionaries were the chief victims. Miss Jessie Gregg, another member of the China Inland Mission, we were told (though not by one of her colleagues) had had her head laid upon the block nine times, and as many times the hand of the executioner was stayed by an unseen power. Her life was spared for evangelistic service all through that great land whose provinces she visited, one after another for years. She has many souls for her hire.

Among others who suffered were the Rev. A. E. Glover and his wife and children, and the record he wrote of those terrible days, *A Thousand Miles of Miracle in China*, has been blessed to many who through that book volunteered for service in China. It is still true that the blood of the martyrs is the seed of the Church. As this was true in the Boxer Uprising, so it is to-day, and while the "preaching of the Cross is to them that perish foolishness, it is to them that are being saved the power of God." From mission fields come the glad tidings of heaven-sent revival, brought down through persistent importunate prayer. "Though the shouting and the tumult die," a broken and contrite heart still stands as the prerequisite for effective service for God—for Him "who so loved the world that he gave his only begotten Son, that whosoever believeth in him should not perish but have everlasting life."

Late in July some of the more courageous missionaries had ventured to the mountain resort of Kuling, the trouble in Shanghai having abated to some extent.

On August 21 an appeal came from there which ran as follows:

"The meetings conducted in the Union Church, Shanghai, under the auspices of the World-Wide Revival Prayer Movement have been attended by crowds. Wonderful answers to prayer have been manifested and a great spiritual blessing experienced. The Kuling Branch of the Bible Union of China requests that the community whether in their homes or en route observe Tuesday, August 25, as a day of fasting and prayer that this blessing may go throughout the land and that the Spirit of God may prevail over the disturbed conditions."

The Rev. Hugh W. White, now editor of *The China Fundamentalist*, was the prime mover in the action taken and has ever since continued to show a lively interest in this Movement. He once wrote to me, "You are on the right track; revival is the only solution for the world unrest." We accordingly met on the day indicated for the purpose of joining in the divine call, and again Mr. Saunders appeared on the programme, which was divided into periods of one hour, different ones speaking briefly, and then all giving themselves to prayer. Some sequels to this effort, well worth recording for the showing forth to His honour and praise, I must tell later.

The following notice appeared in the *North China Daily News* of August 22, 1935:

"The meetings for Chinese are still continued in the Church. There is no leader now, but so many are eager to testify of the blessing received or to break forth into prayer that the proceedings never drag.

These are not the least remarkable of the series of meetings that have been held. To a casual visitor there seems nothing to attract the people, and yet they come from long distances night after night (half-past four to six o'clock), even in wet weather; so it is evident that many are still receiving help in thus gathering for prayer."

But we must make one exception to this notice. The Holy Spirit has been the Leader of these meetings and all pertaining thereto. "They saw no man save Jesus only." Our prayer from the very first was that His human instruments be hid; and the recognized Leadership be that of the Holy Spirit. Dr. Howden urged his hearers to give over "the whole bunch of keys" to the Lord, not reserving even a tiny little one which would give entrance to a small room reserved for *self*.

From the *North China Daily News* of September 5, 1925, we quote the following:

"The remarkable meetings of Chinese Christians which have been held in the Church for six weeks (which were preceded by the Missionary Conference of three weeks), have now come to a close; at least so far as Union Church is concerned. We are extremely glad that we have been able to place our Church at the disposal of our Chinese brethren and sisters for those services. We have been repaid many times over by seeing their earnestness and enthusiasm and noting how all bitterness and even national feeling was swallowed up in the tide of spiritual blessing."

The present situation presents a challenge to the whole Church of Christ. Let us "buy up the opportunity" for Him, "to whom all power has been given in heaven and in earth."

As we believed, and this judgment was later vindicated, that there should be no collections for the expense of the meetings; we underwrote the expenses, and a box was placed just outside the main entrance of the church for voluntary gifts, thus eliminating any suspicion of the high-pressure methods which hinder the operation of the Holy Spirit in so many so-called evangelistic efforts. In the days of the apostles the order was, "They first gave their own selves," and when this is true it follows as a matter of course that gifts will gladly be given to the support of the Gospel at home and abroad. Sometimes the success of present-day campaigns is gauged not by the imperishable souls saved but by the number of dollars received.

At the close of the Chinese Conference the receptacle for gifts was emptied, and the Rev. Earl Woodberry carried the bag home for safe keeping until the next day, when some half-dozen of the inner circle gathered to count the money. The Rev. J. E. Shoemaker, of the Northern Presbyterian Mission, who was in Shanghai for a vacation and had been active in all the daily services, and who proved a very valuable helper by prayer and good works, had consented to help in the interesting diversion of counting the pennies. I shall never forget a remark he made while we were engaged in "gathering up the fragments," for the money was largely in copper coins of less than one-fourth the value of one of our pennies. Said Dr. Shoemaker, "With the Apostle Paul we can say, 'Alexander the coppersmith has done me much evil.'" But these "mites" doubtless came from persons like the widow who earned a commendation that is everlasting, and perhaps like her had cast in their all. And in the aggregate they made substantial contribution toward defraying the "overhead" expenses. We had arranged for the travelling expenses of Mr. and Mrs. Wilkes and Mr. Thornton, and we understood that friends were generous in their personal gifts to the visitors from Japan.

Whilst there was much blessing, there was also to be expected the opposition of Satan, enemy of God and man. During the conference for missionaries we awoke one morning to find Shanghai placarded with caricatures of Jesus Christ smoking an opium pipe. Despite all that had been experienced of hatred for the cause represented in the meetings, this was a shocking exhibition of the continued contempt for the "foreign doctrine." So soon as we recovered from the impact of the news, I said, "This is only another barrel of water," and the friend who had conveyed the news exclaimed, "What makes you say that?" "Does not this remind you of the contest between Elijah and the prophets of Baal on Mount Carmel?" I replied. Then my friend said, "That is just what Dr. Darrach said." Dr. Darrach was a member of the Governing Board of the Union Church where the meetings were held, and had from the first shown the deepest interest in the venture in which we were engaged.

With such enmity from the Chinese themselves, we had not at first any general sympathetic help. Dr. McIntosh, acting editor of *The Chinese Recorder*, was doubtless the only person connected with the paper who had any real interest in the meetings being held. Shanghai had many "superior persons" who snickered at the methods used. The preaching of the Cross, which "is to them that perish foolishness, but unto us who are being saved the power of God," resulted in the showing forth of strong emotion as sins were confessed and wrongs made right. One has written that the revivals under Wesley and Whitefield were not without features that caused sinners to blaspheme: "Women fell down in convulsions; strong men were smitten suddenly to the earth and the preacher was interrupted by bursts of hysterical sobbing. Very foolish and absurd, no doubt said the superior persons of that day. But if Mr. Lecky and other observers may be believed, it was the foolishness of the Methodist Revival that saved the children of these superior persons from having their heads sheared off by an outburst of revolutionary frenzy similar to that of the Reign of Terror." And we may add this, that there were those close to municipal affairs who did not hesitate—cautiously, it must be confessed—to express the opinion that but for the meetings held without cessation for nine full weeks, there might have been scenes of violence, leading to the shedding of blood.

"Prayer is the link that connects us with God. This is the bridge that spans every gulf and bears us safely over every abyss of danger or need."

VIII

YE MUST BE BORN AGAIN

A RECENT letter from Miss Watson, who with her devoted friend and colleague, Miss Maiden, rendered such excellent service the weeks of the continuation meetings, says Mr. Chow is carrying on a Bible Institute in Shanghai. Last year he had about 200 students. The story of his conversion in the summer of 1925 gives a graphic picture of the state of a man without Christ and without God. It was first published in *Long Distance Calls*, and as that book is now out of print we venture to include it here.

Those who have read the foregoing will recall the truly marvellous way in which, when the very real problem of securing an interpreter arose, God answered prayer and by His Spirit searched the great Province of Shantung for the one He had indicated, as we knelt before Him a little group in our drawing-room in Dixwell Road; and how (again divinely guided) we were sent to Kiangwan, where we found Evangelist Leland Wang, who had arrived *two minutes* before. The following adds another chapter to a story without an end, and is part of an address given by Mr. A. T. Y. Chow before a missionary society in New York:

"I have been connected with the Christian Church for about twenty-eight years, but it is not quite three years as yet since I definitely accepted Christ as my personal Saviour and had the Holy Spirit to bear witness with my spirit that I am a child of God (Rom. 8. 16).

"I was brought up in Christian schools under very orthodox teaching, used to teach the Bible to students and preach in Church, but I had no living faith, and all my twenty-five years as a Church member were spent in speculation and uncertainty, being for the most time tossed about in the stormy sea of doubt. Sometimes I even doubted the spirituality of man and the existence of God, and it was not very long before I was converted, as I had studied and observed more, that I was able to come to a conclusion that man is not mere matter, that besides this material world in which we find ourselves there must be a spiritual world in which there lives a God who is the first cause of all causes and the governing force of all forces and activities in the universe. Still I could not believe in the personal God and His plan of salvation for man as set forth in the Bible and believed by the average Christian. My conception of Jesus was that He was a great sage who actually practised what He taught and set an unsurpassing example of absolute righteousness by His death on the cross. My interpretations of the Bible were very much the same as those of the modernists, although I had never been under modernistic teaching. But I was not quite satisfied with my religion, and was always seeking after something to satisfy my heart. Being tired of the dogmas of the orthodox preachers and teachers, and the Bible being a sealed book to me, I had attempted a peep into some other religions in quest of that something. But ere I was drifted far away with them, I found out the vanity of their doctrines, despite that their refined literature and mystic ideas rather appealed to me. This set me back to my old study of Christianity. Not being able to see any new light in the Bible by myself, again I took interest in discussing doctrines with the Christian leaders and in attending religious meetings, expecting something to satisfy, but was met with not much better satisfaction, although as I look back now, the certainty and vividness with which some of my friends told of their conviction and their faith did leave a deep impression in my mind, for they seemed to know in whom they had believed.

"To make a long story short, let me briefly tell about the occasion on which I was definitely converted to the faith, at the threshold of which I had been loitering for a quarter of a century.

"In the summer of 1925, I had made arrangements with an intimate friend to spend our vacation together in Tsingtao, a fine summer resort. Unexpectedly, my friend had to leave Shanghai about one week before I could finish my work in my school. I was very sorry about that, as I knew that I could not enjoy my trip if I had to travel without his company, not knowing that it was the Lord's planning to save me that I was left behind at Shanghai, for on the very next Sunday morning after my friend had gone, I heard an announcement in my church that from the following Monday on there were to be some revival meetings in the Union Church, to be conducted by some exception-ally good preachers, specially invited from abroad to hold conferences at Peitaiho and Kuling, where the missionaries and other important church leaders of China gather for the hot season, but on account of the political situation in the interior just after the May 30 trouble, the meetings were to be held in Shanghai, a special privilege for the Shanghai people; so all the members of the church were urged to attend those meetings. I took great interest in the announcement, secretly hoping that those speakers, so highly spoken of, might perhaps help me out of my troubles. But the first day I attended the meetings, I was greatly disappointed, for the speaker, Mr. Paget Wilkes, spoke on Faith, the very thing I objected to, as I wanted very badly to hear something rational and philosophical that would gradually, by logical arguments, prove at least the main issue of the Christian doctrine. In spite of all that, however, there was in Mr. Wilkes' message something from which I could not get away. I therefore went to the meetings every day, both in the morning and afternoon. At the time I thought it was his good English that was attracting me, but as I can see better now, I know that it was something else and more than that. Each time I went I expected to hear something more rational, but the speaker seemed to have made up his mind to preach on Faith only, laying special emphasis on the fact that of all the sins that a person could commit against God the sin of unbelief was the greatest and worst. The messages were full of power, and the Word of God that he freely used was indeed like a hammer that breaketh the rock in pieces (Jer. 23. 29), hammering on my stony heart day after day, until it cracked a little. But I took particular care not to fall into any emotionalism.

"The meetings had gone on very successfully for one week, when Mr. Wilkes was taken ill and the charge of the pulpit went over to Mr. Thornton. Now Mr. Thornton preached in a different way, for he did not do so much exposition of the Scriptures as Mr. Wilkes, but in a most vivid manner told stories of his personal experiences as to how the Lord had answered his prayers and otherwise blessed him. And he very often

G

pointed his finger at me, saying, 'Brother, it's for you, too; brother, it's for you, too!' As I had not met him, this set me to thinking a little. But I did my best to balance my mind, by no means allowing myself to fall into any psychological trick.

"The meetings increased in attendance very rapidly under the charge of Mr. Thornton and a Chinese evangelist, Mr. Leland Wang, who had from the very beginning been interpreter and chairman, and always added a few words of his own, which were also full of the power of the Gospel and to the great benefit of the audience.

"By that time I had been troubled in my conscience for several days and found myself in an Egyptian darkness from which I could not find my way out. Oh, wretched man that I was!

"One day, about the eighth or ninth day of the long series of meetings, I went to an overflow meeting which was conducted by Mr. Wang. He used John 9: 25: 'Whereas I was blind, now I see,' as his Scripture text, and testified to the peace and joy he had been enjoying since the Lord cured his spiritual blindness. Oh, how I wished I could see my way clear to have my share in that peace and joy! As he enumerated the sins he had committed, and praised the Lord for having forgiven him and saved him, something within me seemed to be urging me, saying, 'How about your sins, which are enormously worse than his? Do you not believe that there is a God and that you are a being with spiritual life under His government? Do you know where you are bound for after you leave your physical body? Do you not realize the seriousness of your case before God? Why should you procrastinate and halt between two opinions any longer?' As those thoughts were smouldering within me like a fire under a covering, I felt the pain of it, and decided to get near God for mercy. But somehow or other, something was in the way and I could not approach Him. Then I realized the need of a Mediator, as I had been taught to believe, even Jesus Christ, the Saviour who was God in flesh and therefore competent for the unique task which none else could do, and I said in my heart to God, 'Lord, I believe now.' That was amply a conversion in the ordinary sense, but I praise God that He knew that my soul needed a much more thorough treatment than that. Toward the end of his talk, Mr. Wang gave out an invitation, asking those who had accepted Christ as Saviour to go up to the front. One or two decent-looking young men had gone up without much hesitation. Something within me urged me to go up, too. But I said to myself, 'To accept Christ is a personal matter. What is the idea of going up to the front?' That voice within me said again: 'You may be right in objecting that it is a personal matter to accept Christ, and in questioning the idea of going up to the front, but what is the idea of refusing to go up? Is it not your old pride that is in the way of your confessing Christ before the public? Do you not remember that Christ will not confess you before the Father if you will not confess Him before men? And do you know that there are others in this room that will make their decision for Christ only if you will set the example? Go forward, then: go!: The voice was so overwhelming that I had lost all my power of resistance, and after all, up to the front and down on my knees I went. As I had come to the end of myself, the Holy Spirit began to work freely in me; for while I was praying, once more my sins were presented before me in a very dark picture, not only those sins that I had realized before, but the deeds that I had been proud of as deeds of virtue were also pointed out to me as deeds of sin, because, as it was revealed to me then, that there was always a sense of pride and selfishness in each of the so-called deeds of virtue, generally with a motive for the approval of man. Then I became the most miserable man in the world, entirely at a loss of what to do. And I wept as a child for not less than an hour and a half, until at last I heard a voice saying, 'Jesus has saved you, please stand up.' Upon this, all of a sudden, those Scriptures about the forgiveness of sins came to me afresh, and as I stood up I felt a peace and joy in my heart that I had never had before, and that no words could describe. The Church hall, which was packed during the meeting, was now nearly empty, with only three or four persons left. It seemed to me that the very scene of the room had changed. Even the face of my dear old mother who sat yonder in the room had something new in its look of sympathy towards me. As I walked out of the Church door, the little garden in front of the building presented the innocent smile and sweet serenity of the Eden of unfallen man.

"Ever since that day I have my life hid with Christ in God, and of the things in the world which used to surround me in a dark cloud of problems I now command a bird's-eye view. Although I am not quite satisfied with the life I have lived and the humble service I have rendered to my Lord, I am perfectly satisfied with Him, my Wisdom, Righteousness, Sanctification, Redemption, and my All in All. He has been in every detail of my life. He has taught me, guided me, chastised me and protected me. During the short period of not quite three years, He has done many an impossible thing both in and through me."

GROUP OF DELEGATES LEAVING UNION CHURCH

MRS. FAITH CHANG BAO

EVANGELIST LELAND WANG

[Face page 100

"The trial of your faith, being much more precious than of gold that perisheth, though it be tried with fire, might be found unto praise, and honour, and glory at the appearing of Jesus Christ" (1 Peter 1: 7).

The foregoing testimony—unrevised and verbatim— by Mr. Chow answers the query common to critics of revival converts: "Do they *stand ?*" And one who has seen the spiritual growth of such, replies: "No; they keep marching on!"

IX

LONG DISTANCE CALLS

A BRIEF reference to how the book by the above title was written and something of what it accomplished in stabilising, strengthening, and settling faith in eternal verities would appear here to be a word in season fitly spoken.

The winter of 1929, the writer met with a cruel accident—*sideswiped* by a speeding automobile, flung face downward on to a cold unfriendly pavement—supposedly dead. While a sympathetic crowd stood about waiting for the removal of the victim, I rose up and announced the intention of going home. A hurried trip to the hospital and a thorough examination supported the belief that not a bone was broken, though the injury *to* the body was so severe that escape from death was pronounced "a miracle." It was many weeks before it was possible to take up the usual activities in connection with the W. W. R. P. M. A suggestion repeated, that the leadings of the Holy Spirit as told to friends be recorded for a wider circle, haunted my thoughts and at last I had the assurance that He would have an account of the various leadings to go forth in book form to a wider circle of praying friends. "The Introduction" reproduced here gives the key to the contents and explains the urge for the writing of *Long Distance Calls* :

*"Before they call I will answer, and while they
are yet speaking I will hear."*

"Many are the means of communication in this
twentieth century. Marvellous inventions are opera-
tive. New discoveries may appear at any time. The
headlines of the front page of the daily newspaper may
announce a means of transmitting messages even more
marvellous than the Marconi system, and yet these are
but the expression of the ingenuity of man, while a far
more perfect and rapid means of obtaining our objective has been in existence since the creation of the
world, and, like the world itself, originated in the mind
of God, the Maker of heaven and earth and all that
therein is. No man-made system of conveying thought
exists which insures an answer *before* the 'call' is made.
God declares that 'before they call I will answer, and
while they are yet speaking I will hear.'

"The following pages are made public with the sole
purpose of proving God's right to this unprecedented
claim—a simple setting forth of facts which it is hoped
will enlist many to try to get results by the same means,
and that means is prayer in the Holy Ghost."

One of the many appreciations of the booklet ran
thus:

"To followers of the Lord Jesus Christ, and to His
faithful witnesses in the widely scattered harvest-field,
there can never be a story—apart, that is, from the
matchless story of redeeming love—more thrilling and
wonderful than that of answered prayer. That we
have a God who hears and answers the call of His
children, is one of the marvels of our human life.

"When that arresting little story of our Father's
faithfulness, *The Half Can Never Be Told*, was first

published, it met with a glad welcome from the Lord's remembrancers in all parts of the world. Missionaries in particular received it joyfully, and there is, perhaps, no corner of the foreign mission field into which it has not penetrated with its uplifting and inspiring message. Now, from the same pen, comes *Long Distance Calls, in which are set forth wonderful answers to prayer and the place of prayer in revival,* all bearing testimony to the goodness of our covenant-keeping Father."

One eminent Christian worker, who has read the little book in manuscript, is convinced that it has been written at the dictation of the Holy Spirit, and that the testimonies which it contains will give "renewed inspiration to prayer." May that prediction be abundantly fulfilled; and if all who read it draw closer to God, learning to trust Him more and to serve Him better through personal acquaintance with these records of His ceaseless love and care, the heart of the writer will rejoice, and all the praise and honour will be given to Him "whose goodness faileth never."

The first edition was published in July, 1929, and within a month a reprint was needed. From far distant points have come testimonies indicating the divine favour resting upon the message. One writes:

"We have just received from Messrs. Marshall, Morgan & Scott, a hundred copies of your other book, *Long Distance Calls,* and felt that in addition to the acknowledgment we have sent to Mr. Kennedy Maclean, I would like to send a word of personal thanks to you. I feel that the very best contribution we can make to the spiritual problems of to-day, which are in some ways more pressing and acute than ever before, is to demonstrate the truth that God is still at work and miracles are still being experienced by those who are willing to give Him the supreme place. Your books are certainly helping greatly in this direction, and I pray that they may be increasingly used by God for His glory and reviving of His Church."

And from another:

"Many thanks for the copy of *Long Distance Calls*. The book is a very acceptable reminder that our Father desires both the realization of our dependence upon His bounty and our acknowledgment of our daily needs. One's own heart has been cheered by these accounts of His faithfulness."

The book was reprinted several times and testimonies to the stimulus to prayer came from the high and lowly, rich and poor, all members of that company who own Him Lord and Master.

In His favour is life.

X

THE HALF CAN NEVER BE TOLD

WHILE the meetings for missionaries were in progress in Shanghai, a young woman, a stranger to me, called, and after introducing herself said she would like to contribute her services in some way. A little further talk disclosed the fact that she was an experienced stenographer and had been in Shanghai only a short time. She had recently come to China through the impassioned representation of an independent missionary, and after arriving at a far interior station had in some trivial matter incurred his displeasure. Without considering that she was without friends or funds, he dismissed her from service. She found her way to Shanghai, and kind people took her in until such time as she could get money from the States to return.

I was very glad indeed to avail myself of her services, as through pressure of other things my correspondence had been sadly neglected. Each morning she came for dictation, and in the afternoon the letters were brought to me at the church. One day, in trying to give a statement of something of importance, memory failed to furnish the needed information with the exactness desired. I then said, "From now on we will keep a daily record of anything that is vital, for such information as we desire to pass on to friends."

We had no thought of publishing an account of the meetings—that was something not yet considered. Dr. Gilbert McIntosh, a Scotchman as his name clearly indicates, had asked for an article for *The Chinese Recorder*, a periodical circulated throughout China and abroad, for which he was acting editor at the time. He had not then evinced any particular interest in the venture undertaken, so far as we could observe, though not opposing the gatherings in the least. So we were a bit surprised to receive a *chit* asking for news of the meetings. In the many exacting duties of every day, his letter was overlooked. After a week or two he wrote again, reminding us that his request was still unanswered and urging that we submit something for the next issue which was nearly ready for printing. He wrote under date of August 5, 1925:

"While living out in the French Concession and having many burdens on my shoulders whilst in the Settlement, I have not been able to attend many of the meetings held recently. I have only looked in occasionally, but saw and heard sufficient to know that it was a time of real blessing. I wonder if it would be possible, in two weeks' time, to have an account of these meetings for the September *Recorder*. I would like it to occupy about a page of the China Field."

On August 20 we heard from Dr. McIntosh again: "When may we expect the account of the meetings? The *Recorder* is being printed now and I should like to have a copy by Saturday afternoon."

Hastily we gathered up our notes and took them around to his office on our way to the afternoon meeting. Glancing through the pages, he expressed satisfaction with what I had brought him. I had reached the door in taking leave, when he said, "You have not told me what to call this article, Mrs. Woods." On the spur of the moment, I replied, "How would *The Half Can Never Be Told* do?" He thought it would "do" all right, or "very well."

That is how the name was found for the book which has been so marvellously used of the Holy Spirit to stir Intercessory Prayer for Revival.

When the meetings came to a close September 1, we thought that we were to have a much needed rest, and planned a trip to Peking, via Hankow, taking boat to that point and going by rail the rest of the way. But before we could get started, there arose a cry for some printed report of the Revival—as we now thought of the meetings. Mr. Thornton, when leaving for his appointment at Karuizwa, had said:

"Mrs. Woods, these meetings are not a conference; a conference is dependent upon a human leader. This is a REVIVAL. I have never in all my experience seen anything like it. I say this because the people are just as willing to come, regardless whether foreigner or Chinese is the speaker. A conference is dependent upon a speaker, these meetings are independent of any one!"

Again, the "Notes" taken during the meetings, a faithful record of the happenings of each day, played an important part. We got the little pamphlet (it was already named) into shape for the printers, then left for Hankow. Mr. and Mrs. Earl Woodberry kindly undertook the final task of seeing it through the press and then posting out the copies of *The Half Can Never Be Told* to friends in China and abroad.

One incident will be enough to show how graciously this little message was blessed of God. Mrs. Christine Cameron Strothers, gifted wife of the Rev. Edgar E. Strothers (together they jointly represented the *Christian Endeavour Society* in China) told us of an incident which occurred whilst I was lying in the Nanking Hospital with typhoid fever, our proposed vacation having been interrupted. A large company of newly arrived missionaries were staying at the Missionary Home before proceeding to their respective stations. Sad to relate, many of them were short-time workers with no objective other than social service.

In the providence of God, a young missionary doctor was there, too, and was asked to conduct the evening devotional service. After reading a portion of Scripture, he made some remarks suitable to the text, and then added: "A short time ago a small pamphlet fell into my hands; it was called *The Half Can Never Be Told*, and contained a record of Revival here in Shanghai." He went on, "I had not read half the pages when I burst into tears and, falling on my knees, I told the Lord that *I*, too, *would go with Him all the way*."

One other mention of His working by the Spirit. We found that the surest way to defeat the adversary was in fasting with prayer. Whole days were spent in this divine exercise. One such was August 5. After I had sufficiently recovered from the fever, which relapsed for weeks, to go to Kuling to gather strength for the long trip we were contemplating, that of taking leave of China permanently, I received a letter from a C. I. M. missionary in a remote inland station. One of the little pamphlets had reached her, and she was so deeply impressed with the day and date of fasting with prayer that she felt moved to tell me a sequel.

She wrote that some days previous to August 5 she had felt impelled to observe *that day* in the same way that we in Shanghai did. She was living with a married couple and another single lady. She determined to say nothing, but to let HIM speak to the others if the leading was truly of God. After a day or two, the other single lady came to her and made known the same concern. Together they covenanted to lay the matter before the Lord, saying nothing to their colleagues, and resolved to wait and see what HE would do! Soon the married couple voiced a like desire to fast and pray; then they knew that something important for the Kingdom was NEEDED. The four spent the day waiting upon God, without having the least means of knowing that a company of His children were bowed in prayer for His blessing in the far away city of Shanghai.

How much depended upon this implicit obedience to the Holy Spirit, we shall never know here. We do know that the way was cleared for a further working in the salvation of souls, and the liberation of some bound by Satan, lo, these many years.

Sequel Number Two. As we write, that wonderful gift, memory, calls up still another incident of more than passing interest in this connection. We had attended the Keswick Convention in England in the summer of 1927, and as Dr. Woods had a great desire to visit Land's End, we concluded to spend the remaining days of our time in England seeing something of the cathedrals, arranging an itinerary that would allow us to visit several places of interest *en route* to Land's End. We first stopped at Salisbury and visited the cathedral, then drove on to see one of the great wonders of the world, Stonehenge, with its awe-inspiring pillars. From there we took train to Penzance in Cornwall. My early recollections include an opera, *The Pirates of Penzance*, and when we reached that rugged part of Old Britain, and heard tales of the dangers attending the early life and service of John Wesley, at the little Wesleyan Chapel we attended Sunday morning and evening, for the first time we had some appreciation of the opera. But more than that, we understood better, what is of far greater importance, the hardships endured by that wonderful man of God, John Wesley. We could not have gained this in any other way than on that rough storm-beaten coast.

At Exeter we had a wait of some hours *en route* to Penzance, as it was Saturday and, on account of the half-holiday, traffic was very congested. After visiting the beautiful cathedral we endeavoured to secure places at the tables in the station restaurant. Every available seat outside and inside was occupied, and we stood until extremely weary. Finally a seat in the restaurant was vacated, and I immediately took possession, while Dr. Woods stood at the counter to eat a sandwich and drink a cup of coffee. Reluctantly I finished lunch and went outside, without the least hope of finding an empty seat. To my surprise I found an unoccupied space for one, just back of the station door, and promptly pre-empted it. A little lady in black, evidently recently bereaved, sat next to me. Glancing at the book she was reading, I discovered it was the New Testament. Making some remark about the Book, that it was my favourite reading, she replied that she was improving the time of waiting to familiarize herself with the topic she had chosen to present at a meeting at which she was to speak that very evening, on the subject of China.

I said that I, too, had a great interest in that land, and that my name was Woods. "Not Mrs. Henry Woods?" asked the lady. "Yes," I replied, "I have lived in China for nearly three years." Her eyes filled with tears, and she said, "This is wonderful! I heard you were at Keswick and tried in every possible way to find you, but was unsuccessful. Then I asked the Father not to let you leave England without a meeting." She then told me her name was Mrs. Robinson, and now it was my turn to express surprise. She was the wife, now the widow, of the man at the Inland Station who, with the two young women, had prayed and fasted the *fifth day of August*, 1925.

XI

ENLARGE THE PLACE OF THY TENT

THE first small pamphlet recording God's mercy in the Shanghai revival, *The Half Can Never Be Told*, went into several editions and we were considering another, when something happened. "Signs following" of the intense interest many were feeling for a need of revival multiplied. With some which led to the enlarged edition of the book by the above title, we will deal. During the winter of 1926-1927 we received two outstanding contributions to the book as it now appears in its enlarged form.

Dr. Arthur Strickland, who has made a study of the work of revival, has just sent us his latest book, *The Great American Revival*. It is a perfect mine of information, a treasure on this subject. In the winter of 1927 Dr. Strickland had sent us a small pamphlet, *A Revival with a Million Converts*, a brief account of the 1857-59 awakening that began in the Fulton Street Prayer Meeting and swept throughout the United States, Great Britain and many parts of the world. While we read this with intense interest, it never occurred to us to use it in compiling a larger edition of the booklet already so greatly used of the Holy Spirit. Later in the winter, the post from India brought another small volume which we did not open for some time. When we did, we discovered that it, too, was on the work of Revival, a much fuller account of that of 1857-60. It was entitled, *The Power of Prayer*, by Dr. Samuel Prime. The copy was very much worn and extensively marked. It had been secured through the interest of our friend, Mr. F. Kehl, of Calcutta, a warm friend of the Rev. J. R. Ward, of Coonoor, the owner of the small volume. The book was about sixty-five years old. With it came a letter, which seems to be needed here to make the record of His mighty working complete:

"Beloved Brother Kehl: I have great joy in sending you the complete book, *The Power of Prayer*, by Dr. Samuel Irenæus Prime, published in New York seventy years ago. I am happy in the thought that my little volume will be multiplied immeasurably. There must be octogenarians in the U.S.A. who were in that time seventy years ago; and I pray that dear Mrs. Woods may rise to the occasion and be, like Esther, 'for such a time as this.' I am believing for this. Truly it will be a great thing to have share in setting this precious volume on its way to spread the fire of Revival, 'and so much the more as we see the day approaching' (Heb. 10. 25). I have gotten into the way lately of thinking of that day as the day of the three Rs: Return, Resurrection, Rapture; but now I add Revival, a grand quartette!"

Still I did not realize the significance of the interest these friends were manifesting in the theme which was so deeply exercising my mind. The story has already been told of how this last book played a part in some daily meetings for prayer, and the interest it created in the mind of one of the ministers who attended and which eventually led to the combination of the story, much deleted, of the revival of 1857 and that of 1925, the one in so-called Christian lands, the other in the far-off land of China. The latter was even more widespread in its influence, though taking quite a different form.

But the story is still incomplete, for the most wonderful part remains to be told. It was in the summer of 1931 that we received from our friend and counsellor, Mrs. A. A. Kirk, a clipping enclosed in a letter. It had been taken from that great Christian weekly, *The Life of Faith*, and from the column, "To His Praise." This was a further confirmation of His approval of promoting the work of Revival before the coming of the Lord. A dear saint had written briefly of what the Lord had done in answer to his prayer for the revival of the booklet by Dr. Prime, as herewith.

"One Friday evening, about five years ago, I found among some of my old books a copy of *Five Years of Prayer*, by Dr. Samuel Prime. I had read it many years previously, but had forgotten most of its contents. I found it to be the wonderful story of the five years following the start of the Fulton Street Noonday Prayer Meetings in New York in 1857. I was so impressed with the book that I sat till long after midnight and practically read it through before laying it down. I found it contained oft-repeated references to a former book by the same author, entitled, *The Power of Prayer*. Before retiring to rest I knelt and asked our Heavenly Father to send me a copy of that book. On the following Sunday afternoon I went to a meeting of the Salvation Army, arriving about fifteen minutes before the time of service. Almost immediately a good brother came in and took a seat behind me. After a few words of greeting, he began to speak quietly about the work of the Lord, and said, 'We do not pray enough.' I signified my agreement. Then he said, 'I have a little book at home on prayer which I would like to lend you.' I inquired the name of the book, and he replied *The Power of Prayer*. I confess it was not easy to be calm as I asked him, 'Is the author Dr. Prime of America?' He replied, 'Yes.' The next day he *gave me the book*, not lent it. It had been published over sixty years ago in Halifax (Yorks.), and had doubtless been out of print a long time. I might have sought it in vain in the book shops. About three or four days after, when I had read *The Power of Prayer*, I prayed very earnestly to our Heavenly Father that He would put it into the heart of some one or more of His servants to republish the book or some portion of it. Judge of my joy when some two years later there came into my hands a copy of Mrs. Woods' *The Half Can Never Be Told*. I found that pages 21 to 68 were repeated from *The Power of Prayer*. Later, I have been again rejoiced to learn of the large numbers gratuitously circulated.* I can only praise God and thank His servants."

If the full story concerning the translation of *The Half* into Spanish were told, it would make a number of pages; we confine ourself to the "high lights." It was the early autumn of 1928, when recovering from an illness, I learned of a newly opened "Paying Guest

* More than 200,000 copies, including 5,000 in Japanese and 10,000 in Spanish, have been circulated.

House" on Cape Cod. This exactly suited me for recovery, and in due time I arrived. It so happened that the previous day a missionary from Ecuador had become a guest. Invalided home, he too was recuperating in this salty atmosphere. At this particular time I was much exercised about the translation of a Spanish edition of *The Half*. The work had been done by two novices, and passed on by a too zealous missionary as being ready for printing. But there came one of those checks which we have learned to heed, and we did not proceed with the work. Submitting the manuscript to Rev. Raymond Edman—now Dr. Edman—he, though far from well, offered to put it into shape for publication. This he did, and the "wonder of His working" through the booklet in Spanish-speaking countries would fill more than one book. It is such experiences as this, which abound in carrying on His advances against the enemy, that encourage us to press on!

"All my life's whys and wherefores, whats and whens, are in God's hand" (Psalm 31. 15, African translation).

As requests for the story continued, we were contemplating a reprint of the pamphlet, when a minister who read and had been powerfully affected by Dr. Prime's book, *The Power of Prayer*, brought it back, asking, "Where can I secure a copy of this book? I would gladly give five dollars for it." We were obliged to tell him that probably the only copy extant was in his hands, and then he wanted to know if there were not some way by which it could be reprinted. We told him that with the needed funds to finance a reprint of *The Half Can Never Be Told*, we were not prepared to undertake this. "Why not combine the two, deleting much detail that is not needed for the testimony presented?" queried the pastor. We consented to think and pray about his suggestion, and finally came to the conclusion that this could be undertaken. Wholly ignorant of the procedure connected with the publication of a real book—a very important consideration being the cost, for we proposed to make it, as we had the first, "without money and without price"— and knowing no publishers personally, we sought the solution to this very real problem. Just as I was feeling too weary in mind to think further, the telephone rang, and a voice said, "This is Peter Stam. I have come down to Ventnor unexpectedly, and would like to call to see you before I return to Philadelphia." As far as I was concerned, he could not come too soon, and I believe I said so. Very soon he arrived, and I poured out my problem into a sympathetic and understanding ear. The great question was that of a publisher for the booklet, now a fact settled in my mind. At this time Mr. Stam was connected with the *Sunday School Times* publishing department—publishers of *A Scientific Investigation of the Old Testament*, by Dr. Robert Dick Wilson, copies of which we had secured for distribution among theological students, ministers, and missionaries. He explained that this department was about to be discontinued. "But," said he, "I can recommend the very company which will do the work. I have known the personnel there for some years, and I am sure you would find them satisfactory in every particular, *The Evangelical Press*, at Harrisburg, Pa."

My burden lifted. God sent His messenger when He knew I could bear no more. Before long the manuscript was in the hands of the printers. A first edition of 5,000 copies was exhausted within a very short time, so acceptable was the story of God's answers to prayer, and, as mentioned before, eventually two hundred thousand copies were published.

Mrs. Caroline Atwater Mason, authoress of *The Highway*, wrote:

"It is long since the beautiful copy in leather of *The Half Can Never Be Told* with my name on the cover reached me. But I will make no excuses, knowing perfectly that you will have made them all already in your heart for me. The book is *wonderful*. We live in the Valley of the Shadow [her husband died soon after this], but here our Lord especially dwells with us. His rod and staff still have power to comfort us. Your letter is dear and full of hope and inspiration. I trust there will be a wide and deep movement of prayer for the Revival which is so desperately needed; indeed, as it seems to me, which is the only thing to save the Church as well as our modern civilization from complete decadence. How I thank you for your prayers, also for your help in circulating *The Highway*. How I wish we could meet and talk together."

The discovery of this letter from Mrs. Mason reminded me of another notable contribution in the building up of faith, which with her beautiful co-operation we were able to include in the gift literature distributed during our residence in Shanghai. Through the generosity of a personal friend of Mrs. Mason's, who believed the book had a great message for young people, especially for such a time as this, we secured a large number of her books at a greatly reduced price. "Why I wrote *The Highway*" is thus explained by her:

"Long before the controversy now took on its present form, I had the habit of browsing in my husband's library, where I became familiar with the trend of Modern Theology. I was a year in writing *The Highway*, but the manuscript was in the hands of the publishers long before the differences now existing between the various schools of religious thought became acute. The controversy over the Virgin Birth has left me unaffected, since I believe in God as Creator and find no difficulty in accepting this explicit evidence of His power. It was because the integrity and authority of the Bible were assailed by Christian scholars that the fire burned within me."

Dr. G. Campbell Morgan said of this book when it appeared in 1923:

"I have just read *The Highway*. I wish I could get hold of some millionaire who wants to make a real investment of some of his money in the interest of God. If I could, I'd persuade him to pay for an edition of half a million and scatter it broadcast among the young people of the colleges. The message of the book is simply tremendous."

Like all the books circulated, this volume brought forth many appreciations; unfortunately these went down with much other correspondence to the depths of the ocean. One letter of particular worth, however, which escaped a watery grave was from Archdeacon W. L. Moule, who with his wife had spent many years in China. We presented them with a copy of *The Highway*, as a *bon voyage* gift when they left to take up permanent work in England. As it gives the gist of the opinions of those who profited by Mrs. Mason's presentation of the schism which has distressed the minds of our Lord's faithful followers for so long, and is still "aired" in both the religious and secular press, we insert Dr. Moule's letter here, dated February 17, 1925:

"Dear Dr. Woods:

"I want to write a line to thank you and Mrs. Woods very much for the books you so kindly gave us when we came on board. My wife has read both with the greatest interest and profit. I have so far only read *The Highway*, but I regard it as a most useful book. It is a powerful story, and that in itself should, I think, hold the attention of the ordinary reader, and then in its delineation of the Modernist it gives full credit to the piety and zeal of the best of them, and the motives that guide them, and yet as truly it is shown what Modernism really is, where it came from, what it leads to in the next generation, who have not first known the Lord according to the Gospel, but have only known Modernism. I think the circulation of this book will, with God's blessing, do immense good. I shall try to make it known at home as widely as I can. I do not know in the least what I am going to do in England, what I shall find there. We cannot tell what will be the upshot in the churches in the near future, but we do know what the final issue will be; the Lord will be vindicated, and with Him those who have put their trust in Him."

> " *To every man there openeth*
> *A Way, and Ways and a Way,*
> *And the High Soul climbs the High Way,*
> *And the Low Soul gropes the Low,*
> *And in between, on the misty flats,*
> *The rest drift to and fro.*
> *But to every man there openeth*
> *A High Way, and a Low,*
> *And every man decideth*
> *The Way his soul shall go.*"*

* "The Way," in *All's Well,* by John Oxenham, p. 91 (George H. Doran Company).

XII

THE WONDER OF THE BOOK

OF the almost uncountable contacts furnished through the medium of the World-Wide Revival Prayer Movement, none has been of greater profit or given more unbroken pleasure than the fellowship which began, when we were living in Shanghai, with the distinguished author of *The Wonder of the Book*, Canon Dyson Hague, for many years rector of the Church of the Epiphany, lecturer in Wycliffe College, Toronto, and formerly canon of St. Paul's Cathedral, London, Canada. It was the mention of his friend and colleague, Dr. Griffith Thomas, in one of my letters from China that lent interest to a correspondence long continued, even to the day when he was called higher in May, 1935. Among the literature circulated we had included the very valuable booklet, *The Wonder of the Book*. After we returned to the States, the distribution of the various booklets was prosecuted with even greater vigour, and we had begun to enlist others in the translation of this particular book.

In one of our early letters to him, we had the pleasure of passing on some news which brought great joy to the heart of the author of this booklet. Through that grand and godly woman, Miss Martha Jewell, a copy was presented to an educated Chinese gentleman. Having spent some years in the States as a student, his faith had not been strengthened by what he had seen and heard there. Though he utterly refused to believe in the inspiration of the Scriptures, he received the booklet and promised to read it. This he did, and it led to a complete change in his view-point regarding the inerrancy of the Bible and in his attitude toward God in general. He became convinced that the Bible was the Word of God and became a believer, with its blessed results.

Something of the character of the author, this man of God, as well as the nature of our correspondence, may be gathered from excerpts taken at random from a large number of Dr. Hague's letters:

"I was indeed deeply moved by your kind letter telling me of the intention of Mr. Braithwaite, of the Japan Bible Society, to undertake the translation of my *Wonder of the Book*. I do indeed thank God and pray that it may be used to 'stablish, strengthen, settle' many in that great land. If today I am a never-ceasing preacher of the Gospel (it's a common saying in my section of Toronto, 'If you want to hear the preaching of the Gospel, go to the Epiphany') it is largely, under God, owing to my having read and re-read Bonar's *Brief Thoughts on the Gospel*. By the way, I will be grateful if you will include in those ministers to whom you send Dr. Wilson's books, *Is the Higher Criticism Scholarly?* and *A Scientific Investigation of the Old Testament*, some of our Wycliffe graduates who cannot purchase them." . . .

"I want to thank you also greatly for the wonderful offer of Professor Robert Dick Wilson's book. It has been sent to a large number of our young clergy, and I know it will work effectually through the lives and preaching of influential men. . . . I would like to have a long conference with you on these matters of deep importance. I think I told you that reading, many years ago, of Dr. Bonar's *Brief Thoughts on the Gospel* influenced my whole life as a preacher of the Gospel, and I am so anxious that, by the blessing of God, other young lives should be influenced for the future. It would indeed be a great pleasure for myself and my wife to meet you. I have often longed to go to Atlantic City, but lack of time and money have prevented me. Perhaps in the spring I may be able to come down, but if you and your husband ever come to Toronto, be sure and let me know."

In the spring of 1929 Dr. Hague, who had just given a series of lecture at one of the Southern Presbyterian Theological Seminaries, wrote to ask if it would be possible for us to supply copies of his book to the students of this School of the Prophets. These we were able to furnish, though the gift depleted our stock, and another reprint was immediately needed. In response to this gift, Dr. Hague wrote, May 31, 1929:

"My heart was made very happy by your letter. I do think that *The Wonder of the Book* has a message for today and especially for young ministers, theological students and Sunday-school teachers, and I would thank God indeed and take courage if a new edition were brought out. May our gracious Father rightly bless you in your large and far-reaching plans for His glory (for who can tell what influential career may be started by reading some of these books), and give you, if it is His will, new strength and cheer."

Two letters from Toronto, dated March 20 and April 20, 1934, ran thus:

"I do hope that you are well, as I have not heard from you for some time, and the work is going on to God's glory. I often think of those words and ponder upon them in the Greek, which I love, Hebrews 10. 36: 'You have need of patience,' a wonder word of Paul's, implying the ability to hold on and to bear up under heavy burdens with constancy and persevering courage. There is the added idea also of sticking to it when others slack or quit or shrink back through cowardice or lay down the flag. Verses 38, 39."

"How can I thank you for your invaluable gift of another one hundred copies of the booklets. I will, with great care, distribute them among the students of Wycliffe College and trust that they will be a blessing beyond all we can ask or think. I am sure, too, the wonderful story of Miss Monson's experience will not only be a witness to God's faithfulness but will awaken in them the longing to give themselves in fullest consecration to God and the mission fields. May God bless you and your good husband and all that you do, in these trying days and very testing, when the enemy is coming in like a flood in colleges, episcopates and church papers."

About six years after we returned to the States after an absence of five years, we received from Miss Ruth Paxson, Shanghai, a pamphlet containing a remarkable testimony to God's faithfulness as experienced by Miss Marie Monson, a missionary belonging to the Norwegian Lutheran Missionary Society, who, on her way to fill an evangelist engagement, was captured by pirates and held for twenty-three days upon a ship controlled by these wicked men. Her deliverance was quite as great a miracle as those recorded in the Bible. Personally, we would prefer to be cast into a den of lions as was Daniel, to being at the mercy of those god-less, desperate Chinese bandits. The same power that closed the mouths of the lions protected the life of this brave woman. It is said that a man was once asked, "Why was it that the lions did not eat Daniel?" His reply was, "Because Daniel was three parts backbone and the other part grit." And the same composition marks the preservation of many missionaries and other followers of the Lord Jesus Christ.

To establish in the minds of the readers my reason for so expressing myself regarding Daniel and the lions, let me give here just one experience contained in *Resting in God's Faithfulness* :

"When the ammunition came, it was brought into the cabin next to mine on the left-hand side, and I heard a voice saying, 'Lock the foreigner's door.' They evidently didn't want me to see how much ammunition they had. 'Shut the door and lock it.' It was shut and they tried to lock it; but the key broke as they tried to turn it. Two hours after that, my door having been opened again, I saw two of these robbers stand-ing outside looking into my cabin, two of those vile-looking men. I have seen quite a few robbers down in Honan, but I have never seen more vile-looking men than those two. One pushed the other one into my cabin and shut the door and tried to lock it, but the key had broken. There was the man in that little cabin; I felt the devil himself was there. His face and neck and hands were all covered with hideous sores, open sores. He sat down on my suitcase, almost breathing in my face. I repeated the promise that had been very precious to me many times down in our robber province: 'The angel of the Lord encampeth round about them that fear him, and delivereth them.' And there was another promise I went over that moment, 'The Lord is like a wall of fire round about his people.' Round about me. Once when I had to travel through a robber district, the night before, the Lord allowed me to see it. I suddenly awoke and it seemed to me the roof was lifted off the house and I saw a wall of fire higher than the house, round about me, and I heard a voice saying, 'The Lord is like a wall of fire round about his people.' I could see the arrows coming from the outside, arrows without number, and I could see the flames consuming them and not a single one passed that wall of fire round about me. I had known these words for years and years, but I had not known what they meant before that time. So I claimed the promise that He would be like a wall of fire round about me then, and that vile man sitting there was up against the wall before he could touch me. I started the conversation. 'Is your mother still living?'* 'Yes,' he said. 'How old is she?' He told me. 'Well, she is about my age.' I asked him about his father and the rest of the family, and we had a good long talk together. I had asked him to open the door and he obeyed me. It could not be locked. I found out that he knew a missionary, and he said about him, 'Truly he is a good man; there is no better man in this world.' He knew some real Christians, too.

* *A mother in China is greatly respected, almost venerated,* and this question undoubtedly had a powerful influence on that vile man.

I believed we talked together for an hour, and when he went out he had tears in his eyes, and he went out very quietly indeed. I never saw him again near my door."

The story of Miss Monson's experiences during those twenty-three days, entitled, *Resting in God's Faithful-ness*, we combined with Dr. Hague's *The Wonder of the Book*.

Professor A. D. Daniel, of Forman Christian College, Lahore, Punjab, India, wrote of this combination of of the two:

"You will be glad to hear that I am distributing copies of the book with prayerful discrimination. The two parts form a happy combination. The logic of argument is so well buttressed by the logic, the irre-futable logic, of personal testimony. May the Lord bless each copy to the conversion of more lost souls."

Our one and only meeting with Dr. Hague, though this pleasure had been more than once promised and as often deferred, came in the autumn of 1934. In pass-ing through Toronto, though arriving late on Saturday evening, I consulted the newspaper, and learned that the pastor of the famous Knox Presbyterian Church had invited my old and valued friend Dr. Hague to address a specially arranged meeting of the members of the Inter-Varsity Fellowship at the morning service. Accordingly I went there and, arriving a bit early, asked if Dr. Hague had yet come. I learned that he was with the pastor in the vestry, and I asked an usher to take my card to him. In a short time the two

I

distinguished gentlemen appeared in the pulpit, and certainly I was not prepared for what followed. The preliminaries being over, Dr. Hague rose to speak, but before doing so he advanced a few steps and, holding up the inoffensive bit of cardboard, said, "I have in my hand the name of Mrs. Henry M. Woods, of Ventnor, N.J., who is here this morning. Mrs. Woods, the founder of The World-Wide Revival Prayer Movement, is doing one of the greatest pieces of work for the Kingdom now going on, and I shall be most happy to meet her at the close of this service." Waiting until he should have greeted the body of students who were present and who were eager to shake his hand after the service, I went forward, but the promised greeting seemed a bit lacking in cordiality until I mentioned my name. Then his face lighted up and he showed distinct surprise, offering as a sort of an apology for the hesitancy that marked his attitude, that all through the sermon he had been scanning the audience trying to locate his visitor, and confessing that he had looked for a short, dumpy and (though he did not say so, his manner of speaking implied it) a dowdy person, while he stood looking *up* at me a good three inches taller than himself—and I was fairly well clothed! Mrs. Hague was with him and we had a very pleasant chat. The next day he came to the hotel to have a real visit ; the day was wet and he explained that Mrs. Hague could not come on that account. He was not large in stature, but in every other way, heart, mind, culture, he was a giant.

Among his last communications, he appealed for literature to be used during the Week of Prayer, 1935, in a letter from Toronto dated December 24, 1934:

"I do hope you and your good husband are well. Did he see the eulogy of his *Our Priceless Heritage* in the January *Evangelical Christian* (page 26), which says it will be of inestimable help to everyone, and that Protestant young men and women on the continent should get it to study it. Now I want you to do something for me. I have to conduct the Week of Prayer services, January 6 to 11, in the town of Peterborough. I will be so glad if you will send me two or three tracts or treaties of yours on the great need of the subject and power of prayer. I want by God's grace to stir Christians of that place. I would so value your help, and I know you have material that I could use for His glory and their edification. If possible, I will be glad if you could answer soon. With very best Christmas and New Year's wishes from us both, and wishing you every blessing in Him."

And his very last letter, which acknowledged receipt of the books and tells something of the blessing which had attended the meetings, was dated January 15, 1935, from Wycliffe College, Toronto:

"It was good of you to send me those booklets and the helpful matter for the Week of Prayer. We had a wonderful time at Peterborough, a town of about twenty thousand, about eight miles from here, and the churches were filled every night and the spirit of prayer and supplication seemed to be strong. God helped me wonderfully, and I spoke on Prayer, Faith, Consecration, World-Revival and other subjects. That was a beautiful letter you sent me from Prague, and it does seem to bring us together when we think of these people in foreign lands praying with such fervour,

and especially young people. Wishing you every blessing and the reality of Ephesians 3 : 20, 21, upon which
I have been leaning very much lately. I like Panton's
idea of the rapidly approaching world-wide downpour
of the Spirit."

Tens of thousands of this booklet have been used
by the secretaries of Student Movements in the various
universities and colleges and seminaries with which
they are in close touch, in the U.S.A. and Great
Britain, as well as in work abroad. Dr. Howard
Guinness, Travelling Secretary of the Inter-Varsity
Fellowship for Great Britain, has presented copies in
Australia and India during tours taken in behalf of
the work of presenting the Gospel of Jesus Christ.
Sunday School teachers and leaders of young people
everywhere have hailed the book with delight. Some
of the inspiring testimonies which have reached us as
to its value follow:

Calvin Knox Cummings, Field Secretary of the
League of Evangelical Students, writes:

"The Wonder of the Book is one of the most con-
vincing and interesting presentations of the glorious
truth of the Scriptures available for students. When
placed at the disposal of students throughout America,
hundreds of copies of this booklet are eagerly and
promptly consumed—so much so that we find it difficult to keep an adequate supply on hand. In these
days when there is so much propaganda against the
truth of the Bible, a copy of this splendid booklet
should be in the hand of every student and every
Christian. Only the student who has been fighting the

AUTHOR'S HOUSE-BOAT, "THE EAGLE," ON THE RIVER JHELAM, SRINAGAR, KASHMIR, SUMMER OF 1932

fight of faith in the loneliness of his own heart can appreciate how much this booklet has meant to hundreds of students in America."

Dr. Albert Sydney Johnson, of the Southern Presbyterian Church:

"I have enjoyed reading it thoroughly, and think it one of the finest things I have ever seen."

Dr. and Mrs. Howard Taylor, of the China Inland Mission:

"We are greatly impressed with Canon Hague's pamphlet on the Bible. We have never seen its equal; it rejoiced our hearts and refreshed the soul."

An ex-Judge of the Supreme Court:

"I have just read *The Wonder of the Book* by Dyson Hague. Please send me a dozen copies for distribution. It is the greatest work yet published on the subject."

Professor J. Grey McAllister, Richmond Theological Seminary:

"*The Wonder of the Book* is superb. I do hope you can lay aside 150 copies for distribution here at the Seminary next fall. I should like to give the book the widest circulation possible at the Montreal Conference, where we can use all you can spare."

Mr. R. Wright Hay, the Editor of the *Bible League Quarterly*, London, in an article in the April–June number which appeared after the home-call of Dr. Hague, gives the author's interesting account of God's leading in connection with this great little book:

"By way of introduction, I may say that in the winter of 1912 I was asked by the West Toronto Branch of the Bible Socitey to be speaker at their Annual Meeting. I was Rector of the Church of the Epiphany, a nearby church, and I very gladly consented. The Secretary asked me for my subject. I thought for awhile and then there came to me as a flash, as if verily given to me by the Holy Spirit—talk about the wonder of the Book. And I said, 'You can entitle it, "The Wonder of the Book."' So it was advertised, and on the night of the meeting I spoke to a church full for forty-five minutes or so, on some of the wondrous things of the Bible, such as its construction, unification, circulation, creativeness, authoritativeness, inspiration and Christfulness.

"This address I was urged to print, and I had it printed as a booklet. I called it, *The Wonder of the Book*. That edition soon ran out, and then another and another, and before long the Evangelical Publishers of Toronto published it in a larger and a more complete form of about ninety-five pages.

"Since then it has gone through many editions, though I may say I have never profited a dollar from the sales in Canada, the United States, or Great Britain. It has been translated into many languages, the first being in Spanish, under the title of *Las Maravillas del Libro*, and then in Syriac, Japanese, Hindi, and Portuguese, as *O Livro Maravilhoso*, and Ukranian, and not long ago in French under the title *Le Livre Merveilleux*. An edition in Chinese has been printed, *The Missionary Evangelist Receiving It Joyfully*, and requests also have been made for it to be translated into Telugu and Malayalan, in South India.

"I can only thank God as I think of the way in which it has gone, and can say with Bunyan, 'This Book is writ in such a Dialect, as may the minds of listless men affect: It seems a novelty, and yet contains nothing but sound and honest Gospel strains.' I am especially indebted to Mrs. Henry Woods, of the World-Wide Revival Prayer Movement, Atlantic City, N.J., U.S.A., who has been indefatigable in spreading it abroad, and whose enthusiasm has been the means of its translation and circulation in many lands."

To date, over 55,000 copies of this little book, not including translations, have been put into circulation. And if, as some believe, those who have been called higher know what is going on here below, this faithful servant of the Most High is rejoicing in the translation of his booklet in Greek by a fellow Christian on the Island of Cyprus, the place given as the birthplace of the Apostle Barnabas. Let us see what the Word says about the work of the Holy Spirit in the early Church: "As they (members of the Church) ministered to the Lord, and fasted, the Holy Ghost said, Separate me Barnabas and Saul for the work whereunto I have called them. And when they had fasted and prayed, and laid their hands on them, they sent them away. So they, being *sent forth by the Holy Ghost*, departed." How different from the present-day procedure! And yet it is the only way to lay up treasure in heaven, "where neither moth nor rust doth corrupt, and where thieves do not break through and steal."

XIII

HOW IT HAPPENED

IN one form or another, that has been asked again and again. Some years ago, at a Summer Conference, Rev. Isaac Page, one of the Field Secretaries of the China Inland Mission, was introduced to me. His first words, after making sure of my identity, were, "Mrs. Woods, I should like to know how you happened to circulate copies of the book, *Hudson Taylor*. I have just visited The Prairie Bible Institute in Alberta, Canada, and found the keenest interest in missionary work, due to the students having received copies of the book. Several have already offered for service in the foreign field, as a result. And from the Principal of this school, Mr. Maxwell, we heard later that eight of the graduates had gone to China and three to Africa." It will therefore be seen that the China Inland Mission was not the only field to profit by this venture of faith.

The vision of World-Wide Revival must of necessity embrace the great foreign Mission fields, where the labourers are so few and the ripening harvest so great. As the years passed, we were more and more conscious of our responsibility toward those for whom Jesus Christ had died and who are still ignorant of the redemption price having been fully paid; they are "without hope and without God" because the Church which our Lord established before He returned to the Father has failed in the fulfilment of her commission: "Go ye therefore, and make disciples of all the nations, baptizing them in the name of the Father and of the Son and of the Holy Ghost; teaching them to observe all things whatsoever I have commanded you; and lo, I am with you." What a partnership! And what a fearful condemnation to the Church which He purchased with His own blood, that in this Twentieth Century, 2,000 years after He spoke those momentous words, millions are still in darkness, and millions pass every day into an endless eternity without having heard that Christ died for our sins.

While there are those who carefully explain that the words, "Ask of me, I shall give thee the heathen for thine inheritance, and the uttermost parts of the earth for thy possession" (Psalm 2 : 8), do not mean what they imply, plainly and explicitly, we believe that God meant just what HE said; and by prayer we can claim the fulfilment of these gracious words. So when we began to think more especially of the great unreached multitudes in the regions beyond, a seed, though long dormant, began to sprout.

One of the pleasures we frequently enjoyed, after coming home, was to sit under the evening lamp, while one or the other read from Mrs. Howard Taylor's record of the *Life and Work of Dr. Hudson Taylor*, the founder of the China Inland Mission, and almost invariably, as the book was closed for the time being, my husband would say, "With the exception of the Bible and *Pilgrim's Progress*, this book has been of the greatest personal blessing to me."

It was therefore not strange that when we felt the time approaching for the circulation of a missionary biography, our thoughts should turn in the direction of this book. Much prayer was made, for there were considerations of no mean importance—the greatest hindrance being the high price of the volumes. That seemed prohibitive, but we have so often proved that our God can and does make a way in the wilderness and rivers in the desert, that we did not cast about for something more within natural means, but while waiting for a more sure word from Him the embryonic desire took shape. We had been called to England during the summer of 1929 to complete the preparations for the publication of *Long Distance Calls*, and with the matter very much to the fore in our thoughts of reaching the student body with a missionary message, went to Keswick. The Convention was about half over when we arrived, but it was for that we had gone.

The Rev. J. Russell Howden, a member of the British Council of the China Inland Mission, is one of the most acceptable speakers at this great gathering, year after year, and it was with the thought of seeing him and seeking his advice that we were there. Dispatching a note, I waited expectantly for his reply in person, and stayed at the hotel during the off-hours, not willing to incur the risk of missing his visit. Imagine my feelings upon going downstairs, prepared to attend the afternoon meeting, the day after sending the note to Mr. Howden, when I was handed his card, upon which he had written regrets to find that I was *not in*, as he was leaving for Tunbridge Wells early the next morning, in order to occupy his own pulpit on Sunday, and therefore it would be impossible to call again.

The afternoon meeting in the big tent, which held over five thousand people, was addressed by Mr. Howden, and though I could have had a few words with him after the service I made no attempt to do so, for my thoughts had not been wholly occupied with the sermon. I was trying to find a reason for the failure to meet him earlier in the day, and already had begun to feel that God must have had a purpose in allowing the miscarriage of carefully laid plans. I left Keswick quite reconciled to the disappointment, fully persuaded that God had some "better thing," for that is always the case. "When we trust Him wholly, we find Him wholly true." So it proved—the seeming "evil" was "meant for good."

As soon as I was established at a London hotel, I sent word to the Rev. and Mrs. Charles Fairclough, missionaries of the China Inland Mission, whom I had visited at their interior station when in China, and very soon had the pleasure of a visit from these friends. During our chat I mentioned the occurrence at Keswick in regard to the book, *Hudson Taylor*. These friends then told me of a new book, another *Life of Hudson Taylor*, a much smaller volume, and much cheaper, then being written by Husdon Taylor's nephew, Mr. Marshall Broomhall, and which was to be ready for sale at the October Convention of the China Inland Mission. This was indeed good news, and as my time was booked for an itinerary on the Continent, I asked Mr. Fairclough if he would get all information possible about this new book and let me know as early as convenient. He did so, and reported back that the price was exceedingly moderate compared to the first volume. As my time was drawing to a close for the present stay in London, Mr. Fairclough, at my suggestion, very kindly consented to approach the Director for Great Britain, Mr. Aldis, and his colleagues, to ask if it would be acceptable to allow the World-Wide Revival Prayer Movement to circulate a special edition of this latest *Life of Hudson Taylor*.

Before leaving London for the Continent, I paid a visit to Mr. and Mrs. George A. Fox, in the old city of Colchester, the headquarters of an outstanding evangelistic work carried on by Orthodox Quakers, whose special "concern" has resulted in an organization to promote rural evangelism. Someone has said, "There is nothing so dead as dead orthodoxy," meaning that a person may be very clear on the fundamental truths and yet fail to function accordingly. The Apostle Paul speaks of some who have a form of godliness but deny the power thereof. There was nothing remotely resembling a "corpse" about the live evangelistic work which it was my privilege to witness in action, for my hosts took me to see some of their workers in rural districts, whose method was to drive a caravan into a farming district, from which as a centre young men and women workers cycled out to the farmers as they worked in the field, and spoke to them of Christ and His power to save, thus interesting them to come to the meetings held every evening where the caravan was located. They sometimes remained for some weeks until a real interest in the Gospel of God's grace had been established and a small congregation of believers formed. Upon my return to England in October I attended a conference, under the auspices of the Friends' Evangelistic Committee at Swanwick, a centre much used for such gatherings, for the purpose of furthering Revival. Ever since then I have prayed for a caravan work in and around Atlantic City, for we have discovered on our drives that within a radius of five or ten miles of this city, with its many churches, there are people who have hardly heard the "good news" of God's redeeming love. We believe that in some way the Lord will provide for this need.

The Psalmist tells us that "the steps of a good man are ordered of the Lord" and it has been said that the "stops" also are ordered, and so we proved. After leaving London we had a never-to-be-forgotten experience, one of the many extraordinary evidences of the continual guidance of our faithful God. Three years before the time mentioned, Dr. Woods and I had stopped at a charming country home in beautiful Kent, England, for a much needed rest, after months of almost continuous travelling on our way home from China, by the long route. While there we met a young woman, another guest, a most vivacious sort of person, of the kind whose personality makes an impression, though the contact may be brief. I found that this lady was stopping with the friends whom I was visiting over the week-end, though the change wrought in her physical appearance since our last meeting was so great that it seemed scarcely possible that my question, "Are you not Miss K?" would be answered in the affirmative. But she was the same person, and after the exchange of a few more words we separated.

Later that evening she came to my room on the pretext of looking after my comfort, for the weather, as is so often the case in Britain, was cold and wet, and then I heard the story of her sufferings since we last met. She had become a victim to awful dreams at night and disturbed thoughts by day. She was almost in despair of being relieved of the nightmare existence she was now living. A friend who occupied a room near that of this lady told me that night after night she was awakened with her terrified screaming, and she was gradually growing worse instead of better. The following night she again came to see after my comfort, and we talked further of God's power to deal with the mind as well as the body. After a time we knelt in prayer to ask definitely for deliverance from the awful power that threatened to rob her of reason and even of life itself. As we rose she said, "I do not feel one bit different," and I could only reply, "We are not trusting in feeling, but in *fact*." I was still in bed the next morning when there came a tap on the door of my room. I called, "Come in!" The last person I expected was the afflicted friend, but how changed was her appearance! Her face beaming with the joy of the Lord and the peace that passeth all understanding, she almost danced into the room—so great was the relief vouchsafed in answer to prayer. After leaving me the evening before, upon reaching her room, she had knelt again in prayer before retiring, but no sooner had she fallen asleep than the terrible visions again assailed her mind. She thought a huge snake, its eyes shooting fire and its tongue darting out in hissing, came toward her. In a fury of fear she drove it away, and with the effort awakened, but again fell into troubled sleep. Again that old devil in serpent form came to frighten and appall her; but now she was given courage and strength to trample him under her feet, until it seemed the venomous creature was dead, utterly annihilated. Then for the first time in years she slept peacefully until morning. Her first act after dressing was to come and tell me the good news, and from that hour to this the devil has been a conquered foe. The unremitting assaults upon her physical and mental being have depleted her strength, but other than that she now leads a very useful and fruitful life.

XIV

CONTINUED LEADING

OUR next stop was at Berne, Switzerland, where
we rested for a few days with our friends, the
Rev. and Mrs. Richard Imberg, who conduct
a wonderful evangelistic work, which includes an
Orphanage and Deaconess Training School. Since that
visit a Yearly Conference has added to the spiritual
life of the community.

Our next objective was the Digne Conference, under
the auspices of Monsieur and Madame Contesse, the
ruling spirits of a great work there. I have been invited
to visit them before I left home, but hardly expected
to be able to include in my itinerary this intriguing
bee-hive of industry with its marvellous opportunities
for preaching the Gospel, which was bearing fruit for
eternity.

Among the large number in attendance at this Conference was a lady missionary from North Africa, and
when introduced to me she exclaimed, "Not Mrs.
Henry Woods?" Being assured that this was even so,
she told me this story. She had become desperately
disheartened in the work, her stipend was far in
arrears, and there were many other discouragements;
chief among them was the dissension and quarrelling
among the attendants of the little church, which had
reached a point where blows were exchanged among

the male members. Some weeks previous to this un-
happy and distressing occurrence, a friend to whom
she had expressed the determination of returning to
France "for good," recommended that she write to
the Editor of *The Life of Faith*, who would post her
a revival booklet without charge—just for the asking
—by the World-Wide Revival Prayer Movement.
She acted upon this suggestion, the book arrived, but
found her so dispirited that it lay unopened. But
one evening returning from a meeting more turbulent
than any previous, and now quite determined to
leave the field of service, she cast about for something
with which to read herself to sleep, for her Bible had
come to have no message. At this moment of
extremity, which was truly God's opportunity, the
Holy Spirit directed her eye to the little package
containing the booklet, *The Half Can Never Be Told.*
With it she retired, but not to sleep; the first page
so gripped her flagging spirit that she read on and on,
sleep was banished from her weary body, and before
she closed the book her spirit revived and courage
returned. She was prepared to stay at her post.
With the new strength received, she went back to
the disturbed congregation, and with joy she reported
what the Lord had done, with the result that the whole
group was revived, and the work went on in a new way.

From Digne we retraced our way through Switzerland to lower Germany, for one objective was a stop
at Prague, *en route* to Upper Silicia, to the famous
Freidenshort, by invitation of Mother Eva. This
saintly woman died the year after my visit. She was
of similar calibre to Pandita Ramabai, of India, whom

I was privileged to see just a short time before her heavenly call. *Sister Eva, of Freidenshort, A Servant of Others for Christ's Sake,* a record of the life and labours of this greatly honoured handmaiden of the Lord, has been written by her most intimate friend and co-worker, Sister Annie, upon whose shoulders her mantle fell.

In the summer of 1927 we crossed the Atlantic on the *Aquitania,* second class. A missionary when asked why he used third class in travelling replied, "Because there is no fourth." We had succeeded in renting our home for an amount that with care would defray expenses to Europe, thus giving us a much needed rest without encroaching upon reserves. The evening before we reached Southampton, we attended an entertainment at which two Southern ministers rendered a group of *spirituals* with such evident spiritual fervour that we were impressed to present to one a copy of *The Half Can Never Be Told.*

Some years previous, one of these ministers had attended either a S.S. Convention or C.E. Convention at Copenhagen (if memory serves us rightly), and while there had come in contact with an earnest Christian girl, our friend at Prague, whose history reads like romance. Enough to say that, having been born into a Roman Catholic home, she found when she arrived at the thinking age that this system did not satisfy her, either intellectually or spiritually. Seeking for something more satisfactory, she embraced Buddhism, principally because it seemed to meet a mental need. Finding this sadly wanting, when weighed in the balances, happily she met a godly woman, the wife of a

Y.M.C.A. secretary, who explained to her the way of salvation so attractively and successfully that she became an ardent follower of the lowly Jesus. By prearrangement this young woman, accompanied by her father, met the young Southern pastor in Paris; they were *en route* to Rome, while he and his companion were going to the Holy Land. The little book I gave him was read, and so much interest was manifested in the story that when they came to the parting of the ways the pamphlet, *The World-Wide Revival Prayer Movement*, was most reluctantly left with the young woman, with the remark, "I can scarcely part with the book; but will let you have this." Let us hear what she has to say as to the impression received:

"Last July I received from my friend your pamphlet on the World-Wide Revival Prayer Movement; I also saw *The Half Can Never Be Told*. Four of us have resolved to give a special time every day for this Revival. The reason why I write to you is, first, to tell you about this, and, if possible, to make you feel glad that there is another Prayer Group bent on asking the Lord to give us the good things He prepares for His children. I can frankly tell you there has hardly ever come to me a thing so appealing to me like this Movement. There are many of them, but almost all turn to worldly policies, registration of members, statistics, and glorying over numbers; while you so wisely let the Lord guide beyond this danger. Accept my thanks, just as I thank the Lord for putting this inspiration in my way of life. May the Lord bless abundantly and let you see the fruit of your labour."

As a proof of the vitality of the literature and its continued inspiration, in a letter of recent date this young woman writes:

"Our Inner Circle, or prayer-meeting, on Saturday nights is, as we devoutly hope, firmly established in the Lord, with half a dozen regular attendants and some casual ones, and we pray that we may grow in number only according to His will. Our minister attends it regularly, and often leads it, and is glad he has the support of at least some in the most vital spiritual questions, as it means a kind of spiritual bodyguard for him. As for me, I consider it the most desirable meeting of the whole week, except when there is the Lord's Supper, at which occasions I always feel especially rich in spiritual respects, the Lord never letting me go away from it without some special blessing or revelation. If I were living near you, I suppose I should call on you every week to tell you what the Lord lavishes on me.

"As ever, first, I must thank you for keeping me among those about whom you are concerned, and for whom you pray. Surely some of the truly sweet experiences of my spiritual life—though it is far from what it should be—are due to the fact that by your loving-kindness I have been linked to the army of pray-ers, and it will be manifest in Eternity when we meet before the Throne how much of all that has been right and true in my life is due to that wonderful chain of events that made me meet with you. I thank the Lord for you, and wish only for a continuance of the tie that binds me to you.

"On New Year's morning we had a good prayer-meeting, during which I was enabled to draw attention anew to the many who were praying all over the world in connection with the World-Wide Revival Prayer Movement, and our minister says too that the New Year would be incomplete without this. As we always have the Lord's Supper in the afternoon, we met from ten to twelve and prayed for you; and that I do too whenever I think of you, wondering how you go through your many duties and burdens and, surely, sorrows and cares, that no real harm befall you and Dr. Woods. May the Lord Jesus Christ Himself strengthen you, and the Spirit of God guide you, as He has done until now. And may all the angels minister to the work of His King as done by you, His faithful instruments."

It was early October before we were back in London, so grimy and so full of interest, and almost on the day of arrival a representative of the China Inland Mission called at my hotel and arrangements were made for the printing of a special edition of ten thousand copies —the price advantageous on account of the large number—of the book, *Hudson Taylor, the Man Who Believed God.* Our only identification with this work was a modest "Crusader Shield" with the words, "Presentation copy by the World-Wide Revival Prayer Movement," a device used to protect the book from being used for other purposes than intended.

In the distribution of literature to promote prayer for revival and to increase responsibility for making disciples of all nations, we have felt we must decrease that He may increase, and with this thought always uppermost we have kept our names and the work as much out of sight as possible. It is easy to see, therefore, how the book, *Hudson Taylor, the Man Who Believed God*, could be circulated widely, and yet recipients of copies be utterly without knowledge of the names of the donors. A special leaflet was prepared for insertion in each copy, stating the purpose and aim of the distribution, but the name "Woods" does not appear here or elsewhere in the volume. Recently our attention was called to what a friend considered a grave omission, that of the name of the compiler of the booklet, *Calling to Remembrance*. But this apparent mistake was with premeditation, for I wished all possible credit to be given to the men and women whose contributions make up by far the larger part of the story. The following letter from a student, who when he has finished at Princeton University will serve in some part of the Lord's vineyard in far-off lands, tells something of how the book was received:

"Some time ago I heard that you were responsible for free copies of *Hudson Taylor*. I want to take this opportunity of expressing to you my sincere thankfulness for the copies which the missionary group of E.U. received last spring, and again last fall. The blessing that it has meant to me and my friends, cannot be fully expressed. As soon as I read it, I mailed it to a friend in Akron (Ohio), who in turn mailed it to a relative in Wilkinson (Penna.); he forwarded it to a friend in Pittsburgh, and it has passed through several hands since. I trust that God will still cause you to be a greater blessing to others than before."

Letters of this kind could be multiplied a thousand-fold. Had it been possible from a monetary standard, many more copies could have been circulated with great blessing. Hundreds of students wrote quite as enthusiastically as the one quoted, and pastors of churches used the book as a mission-study book, so that the eleven thousand copies reached many more than the actual recipients, a number impossible to estimate.

The Rev. William J. Jones, former Secretary of The League of Evangelical Students, wrote while the book was being distributed:

"What possibilities are couched in the publication and distribution of the writings of God's servants. To mention but two of such works which you have recently sent out to members of the League of Evangelical Students, would be to mention only a part of the noble work you have done. I refer to the little booklet, *The Wonder of the Book*, by Dr. Dyson Hague, and the book, *Hudson Taylor*, by Marshall Broomhall. Everywhere I go in school visitation, students remind me of the rich blessing received through reading these writings. One of our groups has made the book by Canon Hague the basis of their study this year. Students continually reap the harvest of thoughts in the brochure. As for the Life of J. Hudson Taylor, the splendid appreciations voiced by pen and mouth are numerous. Just to-day I received a request for each of these books, and fear I shall be unable to supply them. The campus to which they should go is one which the Holy Spirit has but recently touched in a most amazing fashion. Mr. Broomhall's book has impressed students by way of missionary and devotional appeal in a way that few books of recent years have done. The bread you have been casting on the waters is surely returning."

Dr. F. Howard Taylor, son of the Founder of the China Inland Mission, wrote at the close of the two years which were originally the time mentioned for recruiting two hundred men and women for extension of the work into hitherto untouched fields:

"As you doubtless know, my father's biography, of which you have given away so many, is bringing in a rich harvest in consecrated lives. It seems probable that we shall have between fifty and sixty new recruits this fall from North America, a far larger number than ever before. And if, as we hope, the two hundred are completed this year, it will be in no small degree due to God's blessing on that book."

Later we had a letter from the Rev. William Taylor, C.I.M. Superintendent of Kiangsi Province, with this altogether stimulating report:

"We praise God that the two hundred new missionaries are in sight, to leave the home lands before the close of 1931, and most of them have already arrived. We look up with you for prayer on January 1–3."

"*And the angel did wondrously ; and Manoah and his wife looked on*" (Judges 13 : 19).

XV

POWER FROM ON HIGH

PERHAPS no words can better express the feeling experienced before each new venture in the work of the World-Wide Revival Prayer Movement than those of Elizabeth Barrett Browning, "With heaven's true purpose in us as a knife." We have never consciously struggled against this purpose, though sometimes the "knife" has seemed double-edged and stiletto-pointed, pricking into consciousness the belief that something further is demanded to perfect that which He began. This feeling was particularly strong before the publication of the enlarged edition of *The Half Can Never Be Told.* As we have followed on to know His will the spirit-exercise became less severe, and thus when in the autumn of 1931 we found that He was seeking to make known another step in the ladder heavenward, we set ourselves to inquire His purpose.

We copy here from the pamphlet, *Revival* (World-Wide), circulated in a limited number in the spring of 1934:

"The unexpected and widely prevailing interest in the revival booklet, *The Half Can Never Be Told,* plainly revealed the heart hunger on the part of God's people. Wherever it was read it created a thirst for the 'living water' and a consequent desire to see floods poured out upon the dry, parched land. With the demand for this message unabated we had not so much as thought of adding another booklet to the literature already in circulation, until we became conscious of an exercise of the spirit pointing to an increase, which as time passed became an inescapable conviction that the Lord hath need. This was in October, 1931. During the previous months we had received from the author, Dr. John Shearer, a copy of *Old Time Revivals*, and a little later the writer of *Rent Heavens*, the Rev. R. B. Jones, honoured us with a complimentary copy. Under the circumstances the mind naturally focused upon the two books. Which one was the question, for the time of decision was unmistakably at hand. Our own leaning was toward *Rent Heavens*, the intimate inside story of the Awakening in Wales, due to having met the author, and having been, as we are happy to believe, in some measure responsible for having stirred up his mind to write what he termed 'the real story of the revival in Wales.' One Sunday afternoon, the mind being free to weigh the question which it now appeared should be settled without further delay, wholly occupied with the matter of choice I fell asleep and was suddenly awakened with the words ringing in my ear, 'Power from on High,' 'Power from on High.' For the moment confused as to the meaning of this the mind became fully conscious, and was able to recall the dominant thought before lapsing into unconsciousness, and the book, *Power From on High*, which had been presented to me by Dr. William Matthews, of the American Tract Society, New York, two full years before that time, was brought to mind. The compelling contents had been read again and again, and evidently its contents registered; finally the book was

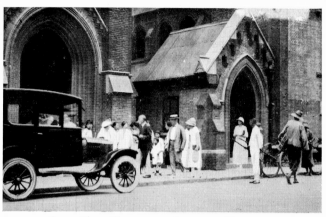

SOME MAIN FACTORS IN SHANGHAI MEETINGS
Miss Jennie Hughes, Mr. Thornton, Mr. Wilkes and Mrs. Earle
Woodberry

THE HOME OF THE W.W.R.P.M.
The friends with us are Dr. and Mrs. Robert Dick Wilson and
Rev. William J. Jones, former General Secretary of the League of
Evangelical Students.

[Face page 154

pushed into the background to make room for more recent arrivals. It had not been thought of, and therefore not considered as a possibility for the present requirement, but that it was the choice of the Holy Spirit there remained no shadow of doubt. However, there were some things to be taken into account. First and foremost, the consent of the author, Dr. John Greenfield; secondly, and of equal importance, the substitution of an entirely new 'Introduction,' for the original edition contained a most beautiful joint appreciation by members of the Federal Council of Church in America; and while we feel respect for this great body of brilliant minds, we see a 'mixture' that bodes ill to the true Church of Jesus Christ. The inclusive policy has no place in His Body, the Church. To His followers the plain command is to come out from among them and be separate, separate from all who do not acknowledge Jesus as Lord and Saviour. For it is only by His blood that we are brought near the Father."

There were other references beside the "Introduction" which we felt did not add to the value of the message for the purpose intended, and at the earliest possible moment we wrote the author asking that all be deleted. Upon receipt of our request he replied:

"Moravian Evangelistic Committee,
September 21, 1931.
'Mrs. H. M. Woods,
Atlantic City, N.J.

Dear Friend:
Many thanks for your kind letter. How I would like to be able to explain my position to you by word

of mouth! Your question leads to many other questions, such as: ought we to sing the hymns, "Nearer, My God, to Thee," or, "In the Cross of Christ I Glory," both written by Unitarians? However, in this matter I have only one desire, as I am sure you also have, *viz.*, that the Holy Spirit may have full control. How do the following suggestions appeal to you?

1, Instead of "Foreword," pages 6, 7, insert Scripture passages on the Holy Spirit. 2, 3, and 4, corrections follow; and the letter ends with this promise—"Joining you in prayer for Divine guidance, I am with cordial greetings,

Yours in His service,
JOHN GREENFIELD.'"

With this gracious evidence of God's approval upon the project we next approached our London publishers, for there were other "mountains" to be tunnelled through, and "seas to be crossed." Both Mr. F. H. Marshall, Chairman of the Board of Directors, and the beloved late Editor of *The Life of Faith*, for several years had been our warm friends and co-partners in the work of distributing the World-Wide Revival Prayer Movement literature. We took our courage in our hands, and asked if the books could be sent out from their office as we believed this would simplify the problem of distribution. As we no longer thought in terms of five or ten thousand, this first edition was for forty thousand, and the reprints stretched to one hundred and thirty-five thousand before we discontinued the distribution. Some copies are still available, though the stock is now exceedingly low, and no more of the special W.W.R.P.M. edition will be printed, unless we receive a new commandment in this connection. In addition to the free presentation copies, Dr. Greenfield has given away a great number of copies to missionaries.

Thousands of letters bear testimony to the blessing received through this inspiring message, and if Dr. Greenfield were to do nothing more for the Kingdom than has been accomplished through this one effort, telling the amazing story of sacrifice and suffering endured by members of the Moravian Church in order to carry out the great commission of our Lord, "Go ye, and make disciples of all the nations," he would have ample assurance of hearing the "Well done, good and faithful servant; enter thou into the joy of thy Lord." From far-off mission fields we are still hearing from those who received copies of this book while in College or University, and the stories of "What God hath wrought" will not be completed until we all meet in that City where partings are no more. The supreme importance of the place the Holy Spirit occupies in God's plan for reaching the multitudes has come as a revelation to thousands, *transforming* the attitude of mind of many unconsciously conformed to the organized machinery of the present church regulations, and acting like a transfusion of blood, for having made peace through His own blood that peace is maintained through the same blood, shed on Calvary for your sins and mine.

With the circulation of the different booklets by the thousands, we had (as we have every reason to believe), in answer to prayer, been Spirit-directed into an arrangement with the publishers, both here and in

Britain, to dispatch large parcels of the booklets from the press. As "orders" are received we send an addressed label to the printers, thus simplifying the process, and reducing the labour at this end. This is needful, for our "staff" consists of but one other, a stenographer and typist, beside myself.

The head of the house of Woods is engaged in special literary work. *Our Priceless Heritage*, published within the last months, has occupied more than three years of his time, and with frequent contributions to different periodicals, and some reviews which are thrust in, and his identification with the Westminster Theological Seminary as a member of the Board of Directors, also a Trustee of the Independent Board of Foreign Missions, an occasional preaching engagement, or a call to address various missionary meetings, his time is full. We both have our special departments of work, and yet in the truest sense are "workers together."

In a city like the one in which our lot has been cast, many changes take place within five years, the time almost to a day since I set out for India until our return in August, 1926. In the church life of the resort this was particularly noticeable. After some little time we began regular attendance, not as members, however, at the Chelsea Presbyterian Church, which had been founded by a truly godly man, the Rev. Herbert R. Rundall, now removed by death. We did not choose this spiritual home because it was a large and wealthy church, but because it was the fewest in numbers and the smallest in influence of all the churches in Atlantic City. Something of the need may be gathered from the fact that in the ten years since our return, the pulpit has been occupied by no less than four different pastors. The one now officiating is a man of God's choosing, but there have been times when the church was pastorless for months in between the different incumbencies, and Dr. Woods has upon these occasions very gladly supplied until such time as a suitable man could be secured, both for the regular Sunday services and the mid-week prayer-meeting. From this church each summer a certain number of young people have been sent to conferences, usually to Keswick, N.J., which is only sixty-five miles distant. Some have gone farther afield, to Camp Pinnacle, in the Helderburgs, near Albany, N.Y., a camp for girls only; and others have received inspiration elsewhere. Nevertheless, we quote the opinion of one young person: "They (referring to the different leaders at a conference) are all splendid, but no one reaches young people like Dr. McQuilkin," the President of Columbia Bible College, North Carolina. Of these several girls and boys, all members of a mission study class I conducted for a time, one at least is studying for the ministry, and one has set her face toward the great continent of Africa, both preparing for service according to the call of the Captain of their salvation.

With these outside interests added to the regular work of the World-Wide Revival Prayer Movement, our time, heads and hands are fully occupied. Prayer is always given first place; hundreds of pleas for such help as is afforded in this way reach us constantly.

The Lord's ways in showing us how to conduct the

work are wonderful in our sight, and are the amazement of those who look for a large office building when seeking us out, and are fearful of a mistaken address when they see a modest dwelling.

But to that modest home come such heartening letters as the following, for both the publishers and Editor of *The Life of Faith* gave us the most generous support:

"London, January 8, 1932.

"My dear Mrs. Woods:

"On receipt of your letter on Monday morning last with reference to *Power From on High*, I inserted a brief paragraph in *The Life of Faith*, and I have written a longer statement for next week's issue. Considering the condition of the whole world to-day, there should be an immediate and a very large demand for this new book, for it is only too clearly obvious to all who take the trouble to think, that unless God is given the control of things nothing but disaster faces the whole world.

"I am urging upon ministers, missionaries, and evangelists in all parts of the world to make application for the little book, telling them that it will help them in their spiritual life, and show to them the lines along which the Bible always runs.

"The Lord bless Dr. Woods and yourself for all you are doing to extend His kingdom. It must be a tremendous joy to you both to feel that He is using you so wonderfully. May He use you and bless you more and more.

"Ever yours sincerely,
"J. Kennedy Maclean,
"*Editor.*"

After much prayer and thought we were prompted to further tax our good friends and wrote to ask if it would be possible to post single copies of the book *Power From on High* direct to the pastors in the U.S.A. The reply from Mr. F. H. Marshall, London, January 12, 1932, denotes the reaction to this proposal:

"Thank you for your letter of December 31. Naturally, Mr. Maclean's announcement in *The Life of Faith* has had the result of bringing a large number of applications from Christian workers at home, and these will no doubt be followed by requests from missionaries and others in the foreign field. We are dealing with them all as received, and I have no doubt that the gift of these books will be widely appreciated.

"With regard to copies for the United States, we are quite willing to dispatch in any way you wish. If a very large number, say 10,000, were wanted to be sent off at one time in single copies to various addresses, it would mean that we should have to get additional labour to deal with the work, and that being so, should have to make a small charge to cover this.

"You may take it that to deal with 10,000 in this way would cost between fifty pounds and sixty pounds. This amount would cover postage, packing and cost of writing addresses. We should have a rubber stamp made, each packet being stamped 'Sample Copy, no commercial value.' At the present rate of exchange, the English pound is only worth about $3.40, so that even if the cost of packing, dispatch and mailing came to sixty pounds, this would only be equal to forty pounds at par, and would certainly be the cheapest and most effectual way of dealing with the matter.

L

"With regard to Mr. X———'s suggesting of broadcasting your offer, I cannot help feeling that this would bring applications from many people who are always willing to get 'something for nothing,' and would not accept and read the book in the true spirit of your offer, and that whilst you would undoubtedly obtain widespread circulation, it would not be the sort of circulation you are aiming at and it would be to the detriment of your work rather than its advancement.

"I may be wrong, but this view appeals to me rather strongly, for I have always felt that you are seeking to bind together in oneness of purpose all those throughout the world who could be linked in this true spirit of prayer, with the definite object of prompting revival, and that your offer would not apply to those who were not in sympathy with your object but who would only ask for the book because it was free. I do not see how it would be possible to make this distinction in a broadcast offer."

We have been privileged to hear of God's blessing resting on the distribution of this booklet, for among others a young missionary in Cundinamarca, Colombia, South America, writes:

"When in college in England, I received copies of your booklets, *Power From on High*, etc., which were a great blessing to my soul. By the wonderful grace of our Lord Jesus Christ I am here in Colombia (under the World-Wide Evangelization Crusade), in the place of His will for me, preaching the gospel to those under the double yoke of sin and superstition. I should be very grateful indeed to you, if you could, from time to time, send me samples of your literature, as is your kind custom to remit to all parts of the world. I should like to thank you, too, for *Power From on High* —*time and time again, with fresh joy and inspiration, I have read the booklet.* Assuring you of my prayers for your work, that you will be guided by the Lord, in selection of booklets on each occasion. Yours in our Lord Jesus Christ."

So the seed sown has borne fruit in many dark and needy places. Surely it was "the blessing that maketh rich" that rested upon it.

XVI

SILENT EVANGELISTS

SOME time later, the eyes of our understanding being more fully enlightened, we conceived the idea of sending single copies of *Power From on High* to ministers everywhere, and we suggested that the envelopes in which copies were to be enclosed should bear the name and address of *The Life of Faith*. The reaction to this proposal may be gathered from an excerpt from one of Mr. Marshall's letters:

"With regard to your letter to Mr. Maclean which he has passed on to me and asked me to deal with as it is outside his ordinary Editorial work, both he and I very greatly appreciate your suggestion that the title of *The Life of Faith* should appear on the outside of the packets containing your gift copies of *Power From on High*, and as you generously give us this permission we will use a little stamp which we have for our use on letters, etc. It gives a reproduction of the title of the paper and the price, etc. It is printed on at the same time as the postage stamp."

We were very much pleased to learn that this simple courtesy had resulted in an increase in the circulation of *The Life of Faith*, but even more gratifying was the opinion expressed by Mr. F. H. Marshall that our vigorous "Broadcasting" of Christian literature had provoked many to jealousy, among others the firm of which he is the head, they having sent a copy of Bounds' book on *Prayer* to thousands of ministers in Great Britain.

The late Dr. Francis E. Clark, the father of the World Christian Endeavour Society, wrote under the heading, "Silent Evangelists."

"I cannot conceive of the religion of our Lord Jesus Christ spreading throughout the world without the use of Christian literature. Since the printing-press was invented it has become in some respects the chief Gospel messenger—a silent one, to be sure, yet oft-times more effective than the spoken word."

The work abounds in romance and realism, for these little messengers of good cheer make their way into almost inaccessible places, so far as transit by other means than the post, to isolate farm districts, lonely mission stations, mountain fastnesses, and arid deserts.

It is no exaggeration to say that to thousands of pastors the message of *Power From on High* answered the question, hidden deep in the hearts of individuals, "What lack I yet?" A rector of an Episcopalian Church wrote, "I wish that I could tell you of the dissatisfaction with myself and this formalism." And another of the same persuasion supports his brother minister in these words: "I can never thank you enough for the little book, *Power From on High*. It stirred me deeply and graciously and powerfully. Alleluia! If ever a church needed an awakening it is the one to which I was ordained. Pray that our precious Saviour will use me mightily. Amen." While a Methodist minister expressed his concern over the condition of the flock which he shepherded in these moving words: "My heart is just broken over the condition of my own church. I have over a thousand members, but most of them have never been converted. They believe in the church, but have no desire for the life of God in their souls."

God alone satisfieth the longing soul; but so many know nothing of desire for God, much less a longing after Him, complacent in their "good works" which do not go further than regular attendance at church services, and an occasional prayer meeting, indulging in the "forbidden fruit" of card playing, cigarette smoking, theatre going, and all other pleasures which pander to the natural man. It is this that makes the hearts of pastors, when they are truly saved, to break with sorrow. Such earnest appeals for prayer and expressions of thankfulness for the help received, come from ministers and missionaries, evangelists and lay workers, from all parts of the world.

The literature has been handled by interested friends in charge of book stalls at the many Conferences both in the States and abroad, and we have heard of remarkable results. Let me share with the reader one of these. Mr. Oliver R. Heinze, founder of the Christian Life Literature Fund, with headquarters in Philadelphia, conducts a book stall every summer in connection with "Keswick," in New Jersey, a place of blessing to thousands. A minister who attended one of these Conferences wrote:

"In some literature which I picked up this summer at Keswick Grove, I note that you have a presentation copy of the book *Hudson Taylor, the Man Who Believed God*. If you still have copies of this book I should be happy to receive one. I have the other books that you put out, and *The Half Can Never Be Told* is now circulated in the membership of my church. It will soon be followed in regular order by *Long Distance Calls*, and *The Wonder of the Book*. I consider these to be some of the finest stimulants to prayer, and to a genuine faith in the power of prayer that I have ever seen."

Some time later we heard again from this pastor. This is the good news his letter contained:

"After having read *The Half Can Never Be Told*, *Long Distance Calls*, *Power From on High*, and your other books, it was simply impossible to keep from starting a movement in my own church, so last April a few of us gathered for prayer; and for more than seven months we have had weekly prayer with unabated interest, from nine to eighteen gathering each week in some home to pray for a local and for a world-wide revival. Last night we closed a short evangelistic campaign in our church, in which a number of souls were saved, the church was revived, and many re-consecrations took place. While the campaign closed last night, the revival is going on. We will continue our prayer meetings, and are sure that God is going to honour prayer in saving souls throughout the winter. This is directly due to the vision your books have given. Please accept my thanks for the books, and rest assured that they are having a great ministry.

May God continue to bless and use you in promoting revivals. Since your movement was inaugurated, the cause for which you are devoting your life has been generally endorsed throughout the world, and everywhere we hear of calls to prayer for great revival. To use modern slang, it seems as though you have 'started something,' and that something is what the world needs more than it needs anything else. God bless you."

Another visitor to the New Jersey Keswick thus expresses her appreciation:

"I have just returned from Keswick, N.J., and have received a copy of *The Half Can Never Be Told*, and the hymn 'Publish Abroad,' by Helen Howarth Lemmel. Will you please let me have three dozen if they can be spared? We are about to resume Cottage Meetings in our house. I am teacher of the adult Women's Bible Class of Park Baptist Church, Port Richmond, and I shall be glad to make good use of the hymn. My daughter and I have had a great spiritual uplift at Keswick."

In the last letter from Mr. Kenneth Downing, of the African Inland Mission, dated February 20, 1936, he says:

"Yesterday I felt the importance of intercession as one of the vital things of the Christian life more clearly than ever before. And in my own experience I know that coldness of heart is most easily dispelled by intercessory prayer on behalf of some of the saints. The Lord has done great things for me since my yield-

ing at Keswick in '32, but oh, how far, far I am from
that steady, progressive life of faith."

At a "say so" meeting both Herbert and Kenneth,
sons of the Rev. and Mrs. Lee H. Downing, received
their call to Africa, where their parents had served
for more than thirty years. Within nine months they,
with Mildred, the wife of Herbert Downing, were with
the parents *en route* for the "dark continent." From
their colleagues on the field we hear glowing reports of
the contribution they are making to the cause of Him
Whom they followed, as missionaries to the heathen.

May I tell you a little story about *Power From on
High*? A friend writes:

"It came into my hands one Friday, but nevertheless I had prepared what in many ways seemed an
excellent sermon for Lord's Day, but as I continued
to read far into the night I kept thinking about the
sermon, and it did not seem quite so excellent as I
thought at first. However, at daylight on Saturday
morning I took my sermon and burned it. Then after
spending all Saturday in prayer and fasting, I preached
three times on Lord's Day on the subject of the 'Woman
Taken in Adultery.' You see, my parish is a very
wicked one, and the previous month I had to stop a
woman who was just such a sinner from taking the
Lord's Supper. The poor soul, though unmarried, had
had two dear little babes, and had put them both in
Homes. Well, at the evening service Christ our Saviour
seemed to be right in the Church, and this woman
was brought before Him. The old Bible story seemed
to live all over again. That very night the poor soul
was enabled to take Jesus at His word, 'Neither do

I condemn thee,' etc. Well, she has now brought her two infants home, has had them baptized, and it was the most spiritual baptismal service I have ever known. She has now the happiest home I know of, and the very people who used to shun her, she now gathers round her fireside once a week for prayer and the reading of God's Word. She has also become a power for good in the whole district, redeeming the time. That all came from my reading the little book; but there is more to tell, for ever since then my churches have taken on a far more spiritual tone, and the Lord has done mighty things for us."

The following is an extract from the letter of Rev. Marcus L. Loane, Moore Theological Seminary, Sydney, Australia:

"I was very glad to receive your letter and the very interesting little pamphlet enclosed, with regard to the publication of *Power From on High*. The influence of that book has been really lasting. It is eighteen months since I first read it, and more than twelve since my friends in Moore College read it, and they all testify continually to its quickening influence. There is no doubt that the power of God so obviously and indisputably manifest in the lives of other men, whom we feel are only flesh and blood like ourselves, is a tremendous spiritual incentive. It convicts and humbles, it awakens and intensifies. It is one thing to envy the wonderful gifts of God to His chosen vessels, to men like Zinzendorf and Whitefield and Brainerd, but envy like that is Satan's work. It is altogether another thing earnestly to covet the best gifts that we may be the best for God—that is the Holy Spirit's work and

that is the influence of 'Power From on High.' I feel
that the more self is abased and pride is dashed down,
and the more a thirst for the glory of God alone gets
planted in our hearts, the readier will we be for that
heavenly enduement."

This letter breathes a spirit of divine discontent, a
very healthy attitude of mind in any Christian.

A Canadian pastor wrote:

"Some time ago I received a 'Presentation Copy' of
a little book, *Power From on High*, by the Rev. John
Greenfield. I laid it carefully away on my working
desk until I could get a suitable opportunity to read
it—and forgot all about it! One day this week the
little book caught my eye, and I read it with increasing
interest and delight. It humiliated me, rebuked me,
and sent me in tears to my knees. God used it to revive
my spirit and re-dedicate myself to the great work of
preaching Christ and Him crucified. I am Chairman
of the ———— Presbytery. We have several young
ministers in the Presbytery, most of them young men
ordained within the past five or six years. I believe
they are hungry for the power of the Holy Spirit, and
I would like to buy each of them a copy of this book,
believing that through the blessing of God it would
mightily affect their ministry."

While ministers of large and wealthy congregations
have been heard from, thousands of letters from
ministers in small towns and country parishes have
also reached us, such as the one here given from a
Methodist Parsonage in New Zealand:

"I am writing to ask if you would favour me with a copy of *Power From on High* and also *Long Distance Calls.* I long for such books to lend out and around my district with the hope and prayer that many hearts may be quickened and refreshed by the Holy Spirit, and sent back to the Word of God to see if these things are not so. We here pray your work may extend in ever widening and blessed circles to the praise and glory of the Redeemer of men."

Another from the Rev. Barclay F. Buxton, Vicarage, Tunbridge Wells:

"May I have a copy of *By Way of Remembrance* and *Then Remembered They,* or if I might have three copies of each, I would use them carefully. I have so valued the other books you have sent me."

A book-dealer in Hamilton, Canada, wrote:

"If you have any more copies of *The Half Can Never Be Told* left for free distribution, please forward me twenty-five or fifty copies. The Lord has greatly used these books in stirring to definite prayer one of the congregations in this city, and used them in a church in another city to the extent that *four cottage prayer meetings were started by one congregation.*"

Another letter is from the Sudan United Mission, Tabanya, Africa:

"My wife and I would be grateful for a copy of *Power From on High*, which we will pass to our nearest missionary neighbours, an Australian couple eighty

miles away, and another couple one hundred and
twenty miles away. May God use this distribution of
your book to produce much fruit in every mission field
for His glory."

Yet another from the Rev. W. A. Hillis, Los Angeles,
California:

"I've just returned from several days on a trip
covering five thousand miles. On the trip I read again
the little booklet that you sent me some time ago.
My heart was stirred within me as I read it again, so
I am writing you to ask if I can have some copies. I'm
sending a cheque for $1.00 to help pay for the postage
in sending them if they are to be had.

"I certainly wish that we might be able to do
something out here. Last year the Fundamental
Evangelistic Association started a prayer meeting on
Friday noon, have four, five, or so people.

"If I could have some copies of *The Half Can Never
Be Told*, I should give them out and ask the children
of the King to read them as soon as possible, and
return them so I can let others use them, and thus try
to arouse a greater interest in the prayer gatherings.
Friends have asked, 'Can't we have another day in
the week?' but so far we have not felt led. Pray that
we shall be guided and directed.

"I'm glad God has appointed you to that high calling of 'Remembrancers' which you find in Isaiah 62 : 6,
marginal reading. It would seem as if God were saying that He might forget, so appointed Grace Woods
to remind Him of the different ones.

"Praying for His very best for you and yours, and
always glad to hear from and to serve you in any way
that I can when you're this way."

Hearing of the great blessing recently experienced at Wheaton College in revival, largely as the result of the deep concern of one of the students, I learned that the name of this divinely appointed messenger, Don Hillis, was the same as that of the friend whose letter appears above. I sent the college man a copy of the foregoing letter, and received the following gracious acknowledgment:

"I appreciate ever so much receiving the lovely letter from you with the enclosed letter from my grandfather. I am grateful to God for such a grandfather. These are the closing days of my college career and thus very busy—too busy to give me time to read at present. However, I'm heading for Kansas City, Mo., to-morrow for some special meetings, and shall take *The Half Can Never Be Told* and get into it on the train, D.V. Thanking you very kindly for the books and for your interest,

"I remain, in the hope of His soon return."

Should we not remember this modern and modest "Timothy" in our prayers? He claims no credit for the part he played in the great blessng that descended upon the more than 1,000 students at Wheaton.

The letters submitted for the encouragement of the readers of this book have been without exception unsolicited, and very emphatically reveal the deep longing on the part of His own people for an awakening that shall stir the "dry bones," which have already lain too long in the valley of *indecision*, to a lively faith in Christ their Saviour—and cause the unbelieving and sinners to inquire the Way of Life Eternal. The reaction to the message contained in *The Half Can Never Be Told*, indicated by the letters from all parts of this great globe, conclusively prove that the Holy Spirit has been preparing a people—which is daily added to—to claim the promised poured-out blessing from heaven. Unmistakable signs multiply that His people are heeding the words: "Break up your fallow ground: for it is time to seek the Lord, till he come and rain righteousness upon you." "O Lord, revive" —or, as the margin reads, "preserve alive—thy work; in the midst of the years make known; in wrath remember mercy." This cry of the Prophet Habakkuk literally goes up to Jehovah night and day, and He will answer and make Jerusalem a praise and a glory to His matchless Name.

XVII

BY WAY OF REMEMBRANCE

THE editor of *The Australian Christian*, a Christian weekly which we understand has a large circulation throughout Australia and New Zealand, reviewed the book *By Way of Remembrance*, a copy having been furnished him by Mr. W. J. Tunley, Hon. Director of The Queensland Evangelization Society, with headquarters at Brisbane. The paper which contained this fine appreciation of the booklet was sent to me by Mr. G. E. Ardill, Superintendent of The Evangelization Society of New South Wales, which is connected with some dozen other Christian organization with headquarters in Sydney, Australia. "They helped every one his neighbour, and every one said to his brother, Be of good courage. So the carpenter encouraged the founder, and he that smootheth with the hammer, him that smote the anvil, saying, It is ready for the sodering: and he fastened it with nails, that it should not be moved." These words illustrate through the cooperation of His servants everywhere God's "inclusive policy" for the World-Wide Revival Prayer Movement.

"There letters gather up a record of God's wondrous doings in all latitudes and longitudes, with and through all kinds and conditions of men who knew how to surrender all absolutely to God, and wait on Him in prevailing prayer, a record of men and women who utterly believe in God. We are told, 'The depression of 1857 was so like the present time, and the people turned to God for forgiveness, and He in answer to their prayers did heal their land and forgive their sins.' It is frankly confessed that, 'Lawlessness is flagrantly brazen in every part of the world; in every department of life; in the home, in business; in Church and State.' 'Modernism is deifying the creature and placing him on a plane with the Creator.' But that is not all. 'The Holy Spirit is working in power in the true Church, and the signs following, as recorded in these letters, are altogether cheering.' We are told, 'God seems to be raising up groups of really keen born again men in nearly every part of the civilised world.' These letters strangely move us, and tell us how 'The King of glory passeth on His way. It is not in one land only that God is glorifying His Son Jesus Christ in answer to persistent prayer, but in all lands, India, China, Japan, Portugal, Africa, and Spain, God is working wondrously.' '*It is significant that the Movement does not stress methods, is not pledged to plans, but to the Holy Spirit, to the living Word, to Spirit-filled men, and to Almighty God.*'"

The letters above referred to under the title given to this chapter were a compilation of semi-annual messages which had been issued for some four years previously to the publication of the book. Another four years earlier God had put it into my heart to send out these reminders of His working in the different members of the Church, and while still waiting to make assurance doubly sure, for we have a fear and a dread

M

of any other thing than "Whatsoever He saith," and having this assurance we then hasten to do it. In God's time we had a visit from a friend to whom we opened our mind on the subject that had been exercising us. Submitting some of the letters for her to read, telling of the thrill of joy in knowing that they were among a vast company who prayed for revival and not, as they had sometimes been tempted to believe, quite alone in this longing, she exclaimed, "The growth of this work is simply phenomenal—only four years old. Nothing on earth could stop it now. It is wholly unique; I know of nothing that operates in the same way."

From all quarters the compilation was hailed with joy and thanksgiving. Mr. J. Kennedy Maclean, editor of *The Life of Faith*, London, published the first letter in its entirety in that paper, which immediately brought increased inquiries and expressions of rejoicing.

"Your letter gives a bird's-eye view of the work of God in the Body of Christ, world-wide, such as has never been published before. It speaks to us of having reached one of the last milestones in the Church's history, before the great event in Joel 2 : 28 takes place. One thing is certain; it is that the nearer we come to the Day of days, when the Spirit will be poured out upon all flesh, the more the preparatory work will be intensified."

So wrote one of the most faithful and devoted of His followers, Mr. F. Kehl of Calcutta.

We had often been urged to gather up these letters into a whole, for the encouragement of the saints, but had consistently made excuse that they had, we believed, served the purpose God intended, and so the days went by until late in December, 1931, we had an unexpected pleasure in a call from a missionary whose station is in the far north of India, within sight of the great unscaled Mount Everest. He had been in the States during a furlough period which was shortly to terminate, and on his way to New York, from which port he and his family were sailing the next day, he had made a detour for the express purpose of seeing us, and asking that we call for a day of prayer with fasting, world-wide. We were surprised, to put it mildly, at this request, and hastened to disclaim the prerogative for such an undertaking, suggesting that the big organizations were in a position to be approached. Quietly our guest went on to speak of the appalling need as discovered in his travels throughout this country, where he had visited many Conferences and observed the spiritual status generally. "I do not," said he, "see how things can get much worse," adding that he did not suppose that the thing asked could be arranged quickly, etc. It was not long after his visit that we had another which was used of the Lord to focus attention upon the need for a "call" to prayer. Mrs. Kirk again urged the publication of the letters in book form, and again we listened without committing ourselves to the proposition.

It was some weeks later that during a day spent in quiet waiting upon the Lord with fasting that these two incidents came before us, with such vividness that we were constrained to consider seriously the possibilities of action. As we thought of the matter we came to the conclusion that the letters published in whole would constitute the "call" our missionary friend had so ardently presented. In obedience to this conviction

40,000 copies of *By Way of Remembrance* have been circulated. The work of the World-Wide Revival Prayer Movement has always been conducted in the quietest way possible, for we abhor propaganda and shun anything that smacks of the spectacular. The literature has been of such a deeply spiritual character that it has been self-propagating. One of many letters recently received bears witness to the statement above made. It is from a New York friend, dated February 5, 1936:

"Dear Christian Friends: I thank you most warmly for the volume of spiritual fellowship entitled *By Way of Remembrance*. Strangely enough, *I have not known of your work before ; the calling of believers to united prayer for revival in the Body of Christ. This is a God-given marvel in our days, something like the gift of prophecy given by Jehovah to his prophets in Israel, at the periods of her great declension in faith*. Through illness I was unable to write to you before the New Year: my own watch-night hours in my room were kept with you, in supplication to our Father, for a downpour of the Spirit's cleansing and power upon the apostatized and cold and unbelieving Church of the Son (the visible Church; the only one known to the man outside). To my great pleasure, I received later *another* treat at your kindly hands, *The Half Can Never Be Told*, giving a vivid account of your work in China, attended as it was by the very evidences of the presence of the Holy Spirit of God, in heart and word, that we long to behold in the church at home, where only in groups, and quiet pairs, and home gatherings, of God's children in Jesus Christ, the love to God and gratitude of our Saviour, are frankly and freely present. Along with this rare witness to the attending heart of God to all that call upon. Him in truth, came that gem of spiritual history and interest, *Power From on High*, by Dr. John Greenfield. This account was a sheer delight to me; for I had long known that the Moravians were the source of Wesley's radiant faith, and had read Dr. Greenfield's pages on this in the *Journal of John Wesley*, exactly the ship scene. But this book brought great illumination on the rise of this group in Europe. I did not connect them with the famous Gussites; and did not know before that with them originated the precious Scripture studying 'Brethren' movement, later so rich in contribution to teaching in Britain. Dear friends, I thank you for these heartily; but even more of the fellowship in the things of Christ which your books have brought. Yours waiting for His voice."

The letter following is but one of thousands that breathe the same longing and admit the same failing. Numbers write that books have been neglected, until in an extremity which proved to be "God's opportunity" the message has found lodgment in the heart and determination to press on has been given, to find that, as one writer says, "Instead of being alone I found I was in a very large company." This has been the experience of thousands.

"Dear Fellow Christians: There came into our home some months ago a book entitled *By Way of Remembrance*. It came in the mail and did not receive immediate attention. More than three years ago a few women in our Assembly began meeting weekly to pray for ourselves and the Christians with whom we assemble, because we felt that the spiritual condition was low. Later on we were moved to pray that the hearts of all the Lord's children might be revived. One by one, as time went on, our members decreased because of not seeing results in our Assembly, till we were only four, three, or even two, in number. One day much discouraged and feeling alone, and wondering if it were worth while to continue longer, I reached over to a pile of books and laid hold of the above mentioned volume. Knowing nothing of its contents, I began reading the preface, and was amazed. I turned to the cover to see what I had, and noticed the inset, 'World-Wide Revival Prayer Movement.' I read again, and found letters from all over the world. Instead of being alone I found I was in a very large company. I went to the meeting rejoicing, and told what I had found. . . . I want my heart revived, and am waiting for the out-pouring of the Holy Spirit. I am sure that with the Revival will come that love for one another among Christians by which the world will know that we are disciples of the Lord."

Another Christian editor wrote:

"After reading *By Way of Remembrance*, I wish to bear testimony to its great influence in stimulating prayer, increasing faith, encouraging hope, and giving praise to God for those who have supplied such books that are calculated to lead our thoughts to the author of *The Book*, the God-breathed, Spirit-inspired, and Christ-exalted Word, the contents of which moves men to do exploits."

Much later our dear friend Mrs. Kirk, who was another instrument used of God to further the vital work

DR. AND MRS. FREDERICK KEHL, CALCUTTA, INDIA

Their home was the Author's Headquarters during the months in China.

THE AUTHOR IN FRONT OF "KILLARNEY" MISSIONARY REST HOME, COLOMBO, CEYLON, WITH FACE TURNED TOWARD CHINA.

[*Face page* 182

for revival through the letters as they appeared in *By Way of Remembrance*, wrote:

"I am giving close attention to *By Way of Remembrance*, and am amazed at the *facts* (not mere statements), inspiration, encouragement, and reinforcement that have gone throughout the world through these simple channels. . . . Letters! The offers to translate in other than the English tongue. Am taking note of the existing translations! It is like a 'Feast of Tabernacles' to go through them again. It was surely an inspired leading, and gathering them up in thanksgiving."

The circulation of *By Way of Remembrance* brought forth expressions of wonder, love and praise from believers in all parts of the world. The gathering up into a concrete whole of these semi-annual letters, issued over a period of some four years or more, focused attention upon an organism pulsing with life. Stripped of the spectacular, denuded of denominationalism, paying no tribute to those three imposters—popularity, prominence and personality— so highly esteemed by the general run of organized efforts, the book moved His followers to joy and rejoicing, and we were in receipt of hundreds of letters which attributed to the Movement the place of "the greatest work yet known." Mr. J. Kennedy Maclean, late editor of *The Life of Faith*, as one of his last acts before leaving the editorial rooms for a time of recreation, culminating in his translation, was moved to write:

"In these days when in so many countries we are witnessing a spiritual quickening, I wonder whether we give any thought to the *steady work of preparation which has very largely contributed to these foretastes of revival, with promise of more to follow. In this connection it has been my pleasure on various occasions to draw attention to the far-spreading influence of the World-Wide Revival Prayer Movement in Atlantic City, N.J., U.S.A.*, and to the ministry exercised by its leaders, Dr. and Mrs. H. M. Woods, who, for some years, have been sending out *free of charge a succession of revival books and booklets with the object of stirring up an interest in prayer and to encourage the formation of praying groups of the Lord's people in practically all parts of the earth.* It has long been the *heart-felt conviction of these dear friends* that *the Lord can and does use the printed page* as one of His channels for reaching His people everywhere, and putting this conviction to a practical test, they have sent out these books in the assurance that God's Word would not return to Him without accomplishing its appointed task. Through our columns these works have been offered to Christians and others, the latest being *By Way of Remembrance*, and reaching out to those for whom they were specially prepared, they have moved them to *prayer and action*, with the happy result that *thousands of praying groups and circles are now interceding with the Lord for a mighty outpouring of revival fire and blessing all over the world. I do not think I am claiming too much* when *I say* that the World-Wide Revival Prayer Movement, through the inspired leadership of the friends named, *has contributed in a very large measure to the new spirit which is abroad to-day.* If, at times, they have sown in tears, they are now beginning to reap in joy, and are fervently thanking God for every sign of the awakening which is so widely making itself felt."

Words are wholly inadequate to express our appreciation for the cordial and constant co-operation rendered through the instrumentality of this promoter of every good word and work. Long after Mr. Maclean showed his warm support of the work of the World-Wide Revival Prayer Movement, we learned through a friend who lived for some years in England during the great Torrey and Alexander campaign, and others which followed, that this consecrated editor of a great Christian weekly was always present in the after-meetings to deal with souls and lead them to his Saviour. *Small wonder that he entered so whole-heartedly into the objective which has from the first day until now been our basic desire—to point the way for a return of the lost glory and power of the Church Universal and Militant, through the God appointed means, prayer and intercession for the lost.* Certainly the opinion of this good friend of the WORLD-WIDE REVIVAL PRAYER MOVEMENT is of no inconsiderable force. Because of his position, he was better qualified to estimate its scope and influence than any other except ourselves. If what he said were true four years ago—which countless letters corroborate—*how much more* could it be said to-day with the increase in the great multitude which no man can number, who cry literally day and night the whole world over for a return of "the Christianity that always triumphs and the glory that excelleth." Dr. Thomas Payne, the author of a book with the above title, said:

"Oh, that God would raise up a mighty host of witnesses in our day who in the power of the Holy Ghost would roll back the flood of worldliness and religious infidelity that is getting into many of our pulpits and congregations up and down the land, corrupting the minds and destroying the faith of thousands, especially our young men, and such as are not established in the faith. Nearly every truth that distinguishes the system of Christianity from early inventions is attacked. One would rob us of the Incarnation of Christ, another of His Deity, another of the Atonement, another of the Resurrection, another of the doctrine of Regeneration, another of the inspiration of the Bible, another of the personality of the Holy Spirit, and thus one after another they deny the whole of the Christian Faith, and do untold harm to the cause of Jesus Christ. *In the history of the Church there never was a time when there was greater need for Christians to pray earnestly for God to raise up a multitude of Spirit-filled witnesses than at the present day, when many weary souls are getting chaff for wheat and stones instead of bread."*

Dr. Payne also wrote that truly great book, *The Great Force on Earth—The Power of Intensified Prayer*, which many consider the finest presentation of this vital subject yet written. It was among the first volumes circulated by this movement. Thousands of copies were given away, and multitudes testified to its spiritual value essentially, if not exactly, in the words of that great man of God, Principal Edwards, D.D., of Cardiff, Wales: "This book has rebuked me, tried me, and yet enlightened and encouraged me."

"But who may abide the day of his coming? and who shall stand when he appeareth? for he is like a refiner's fire and like fuller's soap: and he shall sit as a refiner and purifier of silver; and he shall purify the sons of Levi, and purge them as gold and silver, that they may offer unto the Lord an offering in righteousness. Then shall the offering of Judah and Jerusalem be pleasant unto the Lord, as in the days of old, and as in former years. . . . Bring ye all the tithes into the storehouse, that there may be meat in mine house, and *prove me now herewith, saith the Lord of hosts, if I will not open to you the windows of heaven and pour you out a blessing, that there shall not be room enough to receive it*" (Malachi 3: 2, 3, 4, 10).

XVIII

STRETCHING FORTH THE CURTAINS

AS we have previously related, the little book, *By Way of Remembrance*, was chiefly a compilation of letters received from all over the world, showing the need and also the tokens of blessing received. These have not ceased. With the belief that not only should our joys be shared, that praise may redound to our Lord, but that these may prove interesting, we add others.

Mr. Herbert Stock, of Toronto, Canada, writes:

"I had the privilege of being in the home of Mr. Peter Stam (Philadelphia) a little over a week ago, and noticing a copy of that wonderful little message of yours on his library table, entitled *The Half Can Never Be Told*, I picked it up and read it. It so gripped me that I read it at one sitting, and immediately came the desire to see if it were possible to secure a quantity for distribution at our Canadian Conference held at Muskoka. I suggested at one of our meetings this spring that we ought more or less regularly to send to every minister in Canada some positive and constructive testimony such as this little book of yours. There are some eight or ten thousand ministers registered in the different Year Books."

The full number was furnished for the distribution requested by Mr. Stock, and in this way the booklet has been circulated in Australia, New Zealand, India, Japan, Korea, China and the islands of the sea, as well as in the U.S.A. It is doubtful if any of the recipients had the slightest idea that the books were a gift from this quarter, and we have supplied tens of thousands of books, for which no recognition was given or expected, our whole objective being to reach those for whom the messages were prepared. Like the salvation of our Lord and Saviour Jesus Christ, the literature we circulate is without money and without price—the present volume being the only exception. Our purpose in issuing *Revival in Romance and Realism*, far from being commercial, is simply to secure funds for incidentals.

"August 9, 1928.

"Dr. F. B. Meyer,
"Christ Church,
"Westminster Bridge Road, London, S.E.

"My dear Mr. Meyer:

"As you can understand, I have been deeply interested in the proposal put forward under your name and that of other friends for a day of ministerial conference and prayer on October 4. The letter signed by Mr. Martin and yourself, in which you thank us for the part we are taking in supporting the proposal, reached me too late, as I explained to Mr. Martin in a letter yesterday, for this week's issue, owing to the intervention of the bank holiday, but I am publishing it in our issue of the 15th. You have also seen, of course, that we are supporting the proposal in a brief series of leading articles.

"My main purpose in writing to you now is to bring to your notice what has been done along the line of preparation by prayer by two good American friends whom you probably know: Dr. and Mrs. H. M. Woods, of Atlantic City. For the last year or two I have been in the closest touch with Mrs. Woods and am acquainted with the longings for revival which stir her heart and that of her husband. Acting entirely alone, these two friends have been so burdened with the world need of a spiritual awakening that they have prepared and circulated the booklet, *The Half Can Never Be Told*, a copy of which I am enclosing with this letter. The purpose of this book's publication, as you will observe, is to stimulate prayer on behalf of revival, and when I tell you that over 100,000 copies have already been circulated and have gone to all parts of the world, you will understand that already a large amount of spade work has been accomplished. When I add that all these copies have been applied for and have not been distributed indiscriminately, you will understand that they have gone into hands that have been prepared to make the very best use of them. It may be that the volumes of prayer thus created have had something to do with the step which is now being taken, and with the call which you have felt led to publish. In view of all this I am wondering whether Dr. and Mrs. Woods could not be brought into touch with your scheme. After all the sacrifice they have made and all the faith they have shown, their labours of love should in some way be recognized and linked on to the conference of October 4. It is quite clear that God raises up and uses the people of His own choice for special purposes, and knowing Dr. and Mrs. Woods as I do, I cannot resist the feeling that the Lord has been preparing and using them to stir up prayer for revival and to advance the cause which we all have so much at heart.

"As this booklet has already been used of God in the creation of a large volume of prayer for revival, it seems to me that this good work might be continued if further channels were opened up for its useful ministry. If, therefore, in connection with the forthcoming conference you can make use of copies of *The Half Can Never Be Told*, I think I can promise on Mrs. Woods' behalf that all necessary copies will be supplied. We have several thousand copies in hand at the present moment and if the right doors are opened to the booklet I am convinced that its ministry would be productive of wonderful results. In our own land to-day there are many earnest people who only want clear direction in this matter, and such a booklet as the enclosed would show them in a new way the value of prayer and how God is willing to open the windows of heaven and pour down His blessing upon all who give themselves to this holy ministry. I feel sure that the revival for which we have so long hoped and prayed will come when God's children give themselves earnestly to prayer on its behalf. With kindest regards.

"J. KENNEDY MACLEAN,
"Editor, *The Life of Faith.*"

"You will never know this side of Heaven all that the book, *The Half Can Never Be Told*, has been able to accomplish. In May of last year I bought some books at a rummage sale. Amongst them was a worn copy of this particular book. I had never read it before, so I just glanced at it. When I reached home I read it. We had been realizing the necessity of prayer, and when I read that marvellous account of answered prayer it was decided to start a daily prayer service at once. This has been held ever since, and God has been blessing this parish in a wonderful way. I thought that you would like to know how this 'stray' copy had been guided, and I wish to add my testimony to the fact of answered prayer. The extraordinary thing is that that copy has disappeared! I have not the slightest recollection as to its whereabouts. God has some further special use for that copy, evidently It is still 'straying.' May God bless you both in your work for Him."

A Vicar, England.

"The books, *The Half Can Never Be Told*, are proving a great blessing wherever they are distributed. I do believe the Holy Spirit is using them as a mighty testimony. More and more people are being concerned about the present conditions, not only in the realm of theology but also in the everyday world. They realize things have gone too far for humans to control them and that the only source of help is from God. But most people do not know even the rudiments of prayer. They do not know how to agonize at the throne of grace. For such who are in need of knowing 'how it is done,' this little book is opening up the eyes of their spiritual understanding. One person remarked to me, 'You know I can understand this book. It has deepened my life because it has shown me that everyday business men can pray, and I am an everyday business man.' I am afraid that too many of the marvellous books on prayer are too deep for the average person and consequently have no message for them. But the little book, *The Half Can Never Be Told*, also has a fresh message for those are are deeply spiritual. It shows them that it has been done and stimulates their faith. We pray constantly that the Holy Spirit will use it as a mighty power for the deepening of prayer-life."

A Pastor, Ventnor, N.J.

"It has often been in my mind to write you, and to-day it is impressed upon me that I should do so. Years ago your little book, *The Half Can Never Be Told*, came to us. I forget now whether I read it then or not, but in June of 1930, coming across it amongst some papers I was arrested, as I believe by the Spirit of God, by that part which tells of the prayer meeting in Fulton Street and the '59 Revival. Then I read it all through and was stirred to the depths as I realized what God had done then, He would do again, and even in this country, if only His children would lay hold by faith upon His promises. In conversation with a friend about these things, we agreed to speak to a few whom we know to be likeminded, lending your little book to as many as we could, and then inviting them to meet with us to discuss the formation of a prayer circle. Seven women, representing nearly as many denominations, met on June 27, 1930. It was perfectly clear that the things was of God by the unanimity and harmony that prevailed. There has never been any very general movement of the Spirit in this country (or continent). I should have mentioned that we are having many evidences of the working of God's Spirit, and a recent encouragement has been the formation of a Men's Meeting at noon on Tuesdays. The work of the evil one prospers, too. Surely never was he busier, but as we press on to learn of the Cross of Calvary and learn to pray from its standpoint, the Lord Christ will assuredly see of the travail of His soul and be satisfied.

"Yours in the hope and expectation of world-wide Revival, including needy Argentine and South America."

Mrs. S. E. Curtis, Buenos Aires,
Argentine, South America.

N

On a Sunday, which we think was January 1, 1928, the ministers of Atlantic City made a distribution of the booklet, *The Half Can Never Be Told*, several thousand copies having been contributed for this purpose. The Holy Spirit wonderfully owned and blessed this effort—some testimonies have been given elsewhere—and we quote here from a letter written to my husband by one of the leading pastors:

"Let me, through you, thank Mrs. Woods for the fine understanding co-operation she is giving the local ministry in the prosecution of the work of Christ. I am convinced that she has been raised up for positive inspiration in the hearts and minds of the spiritual leaders of the resort. And I pray that the city will be shaken as never before in behalf of Christ and His Church."

"The books (200 *Power From on High*, 100 each *Calling to Remembrance*, and *The Wonder of the Book*) were all duly received and in excellent condition. The most of them were distributed at the Convention (Sialkot) and very much appreciated. The remainder will find ready acceptance at the coming Convention (1936). You will be interested to hear that small revivals have broken out in two of our Girls' Schools, the Avalon Girls' High School at Pathankot, and the Girls' Boarding School at Sangla Hill. Mr. Bakht Singh was the human instrument used of God in these schools. One of the lady superintendents writes that she has never seen anything like it, and this lady has seen several Revivals of much power. This Mr. Singh

himself had a wonderful conversion when on boar
ship going over to Canada."

Rev. J. A. McConnelee,
American U.P. Mission, Gujranwala,
Punjab, India.

"I have your printed circular which was forwarded
to me from G————, my last charge on the West
Coast of the South Island of New Zealand. It was
gratifying to know from the testimonial letters included
in the circular that your booklet, *The Half Can Never
Be Told*, had been so instrumental in the deepening of
spiritual life throughout the world. The district to
which I have just been called is a very wealthy sheep-
ranching locality, but, so far as I have been able to
ascertain, is spiritually at a low ebb. Sporting and
racing are the commonest features. One of my serious
drawbacks as vicar of this parish is my inability to
procure books, owing to the insufficienty of my stipend.
I had heard of the books you were circulating and the
blessing which attended their circulation, but I did
not care to ask for free copies. My wife and I have not
yet been able to find any one to join us in prayer
meetings. Our church attendance is fairly good, but
the mere mention of a prayer meeting scares people
off. We hold a meeting in the vicarage every Monday
evening to pray for world-wide Revival and our parish
needs, but as yet no other (except the Lord Himself)
has joined us. May the coming New Year bring with
it an avalanche of prayer and sacrifice in order that
Christ's Kingdom may be richly and widely extended,
His Name glorified and His coming expedited."

A Clergyman,
New Zealand.

"*The Half Can Never Be Told*, I am sure, has done a wonderful work in this country. One of our Bible women, Sra. Irene, has found it greatly inspiring. Recently she has been doing a magnificent work in our stations and *quite a large number of people* have been converted through her instrumentality. I am also continuing to receive requests for the book, but I am sorry to say that now I have none left. If it is possible for you to send me another fifty copies, I should be most grateful."

REV. PERCY BUFFARD,
Valdepenas, Spain.

To show the extent of prayer fellowship, we quote from a missionary to the Philippine Islands:

"I have received the literature of the World-Wide Revival Prayer Movement from time to time since I have been in the Philippine Islands and it has been the means of stirring me up to pray for revival, not only in our particular field but throughout the whole world. I have appreciated the different books, recounting what God has done and is still able to do, in the matter of reviving His Church, and have passed them on to other missionaries. We need just that kind of encouragement—that *God is* able. There is danger of becoming satisfied with a limited manifestation of God's power and not expecting anything more. I should like to request that you place the names of the following friends on your mailing list. I feel that they would appreciate your literature."

From Ralph C. Norton, of the Belgian Gospel Mission, before his recent death, we received the following:

"Some months ago we received from Marshall Bros. a package of books containing *The Half Can Never Be Told*, and these were distributed among our missionaries, as some thirty of them read English. I wrote and thanked Marshall's, but am not quite certain whether I wrote and thanked you. If not it was an oversight on my part which resulted from my illness, because you may know that about a year and a half ago I completely broke down nervously and was practically out of the work for many months, and then when I returned here I was advised by my doctor to be very cautious lest I should have a relapse, and this no doubt is the reason why I did not write you personally. . . . I want to congratulate you upon this distribution of the printed page because our experience also teaches that there is nothing needed to-day more than the distribution of good literature. . . . If the Lord should lead you to give out any more literature, we will greatly appreciate having some thirty to thirty-five copies in English to distribute among our workers who read English, as they need more literature of this character to stir them up to more heroic effort in evangelism."

The Rev. James Worboys, of Sydney, Australia, whose evangelistic labours are affectionately remembered in the States, writes that the distribution of our various booklets at two great Australian Conventions, Upwey, Victoria, and Katomba, New South Wales, startled multitudes into thinking and praying for revival. Thus we have been "sowing beside all waters." We can add, "God giveth the increase." In faith we can leave it with the Lord of the harvest.

Mrs. Una Roberts Lawrence, Mission Study Editor,

Southern Baptist Convention, *Home and Foreign Fields*, writes under the heading, "My Missionary Bookshelf:"

" I do not know to what friend I am indebted for the literature that is coming to me at frequent intervals from the World-Wide Revival Prayer Movement, of 5 South Oxford Avenue, Atlantic City, New Jersey. But I do here and now wish to express my deep appreciation of every leaflet and booklet. I wish also to share the heart-searching messages of these with the readers of this column. The first booklet to come to me was *The Half Can Never Be Told*. I understand there were earlier ones. There is also a small booklet called *The World-Wide Revival Prayer Movement*, the first issued by those whose hearts have been stirred with a deep conviction that the only way out for a world that is lost in sin and a Christendom bewildered and confused, hindered and handicapped by problems and trials without and within, is through spiritual revival, born in prayer and realized through absolute surrender to God of self and *possessions*.

" There have come to my heart experiences in the past few months that lead me to believe there are many hearts among Southern Baptists who have awakened to that expectant attitude that presages a revival. All these I would earnestly urge to write to the address given above and ask for their literature, enclosing at least postage for them. No gifts are solicited for the publication of these little books of testimony and praise, but if God moves your heart to help pass on the messages to others you may share the work by sending more than the cost of the books you receive. All the literature is free. On my desk I have every day the two recent ones, *By Way of Remembrance*,

and *Power From on High.* Other books that have
been available are *Long Distance Calls*, and *Hudson
Taylor, the Man Who Believed God.* The significant
words of this movement are 'Prayer—covenant—
power—revival—expectancy.' In all the literature
the Cross of Christ is lifted up. In all, the message is
this note, 'Nations are in distress and perplexity such
as has never been known. . . . The only remedy for
a sick and fainting world is a visitation of power from
on high.' As Southern Baptists swing into the effort
to provide the money for freeing our missionary enterprises from the staggering burden of debt that is
crushing out their very existence, I could wish that
we might all make contact with this quiet, unobtrusive,
but powerful movement for a spiritual revival. It
would help."

The Rev. Charles Leonard, our friend of *The Empress
of Russia*, accounts for the missing link:

"The Shantung Revival, that marvellous record of a
first century demonstration of Holy Ghost power, had
its beginning in the Southern Baptist Mission, China,
and this work of grace has spread. Halls of Learning
have been entered and the Spirit has laid hold upon
many young promising lives for the service of the King
of kings."

Quoting from a letter from Prof. Kalle Korhenen,
M.A., Lutheran Theological Seminary, Shekow, Central
China:

"God is working through many channels in a new
and mighty way. Now the 'cold' and often purely
intellectual and 'static' Christians have got on fire,

there is a constant stream of weeping going on in China, the motive being only spiritual for the exceeding sinfulness of sin, and consequently great and loud joy in the Lord and evangelistic zeal all over. Many burning witness-bearers are roaming through the length and breadth of China. Under the convicting power of the Holy Spirit, many foreign missionaries have been marvellously changed. Great things are being accomplished but there is much more to be done. These great things should stimulate our prayer life, and encourage us to pray and hope for still greater things."

XIX

WHAT NEXT?

"Delays are not refusals ; many a prayer is registered, and underneath the words ' My time is not yet come,' God has set a time as well as a set purpose, and He who orders the bounds of our habitation orders also the time of our deliverance."

AFTER the publication of *By Way of Remembrance* and one or two smaller booklets, the question was, What next, Lord? No answer was forthcoming, but a distinct impression almost like a voice was vouchsafed that He would make known His desire in His own time and way. In the autumn of 1933 we issued the booklet, *Then Remembered They*, a compilation of letters received from "Members" and excerpts from the writings of men and women famous for their consecrated lives. The former booklets, especially *The Half Can Never Be Told*, and *Power From on High*, also *By Way of Remembrance*, were still in great demand ; as a matter of fact, their appeal has never lessened. To-day we are in receipt of requests for all three of these booklets and the testimonies to the blessing that rests upon the printed page are truly wonderful. No book published by the World-Wide Revival Prayer Movement has been a book for the hour. Again and again we hear that copies are fairly worn out with repeated readings. A missionary from China, whose station is on the Tibetan border, called to tell me that the literature sent to that far-off group is so vitally interesting that the books are read and re-read. "One can take up one of these, and open at any page and get a fresh message," said this friend.

It is just as fatal to the interests of the Kingdom to run before as to lag behind, and we are only in God's safety zone when keeping step with the Lord. And so we waited for the leading of the Holy Spirit which was made clear in due time. In November of the year mentioned, we received from a student at Moore College, Sydney, Australia, a very beautiful letter. It was one in which he mentioned that he was sending a copy of the College Magazine, "Sociates," and that we would find the W.W.R.P.M. mentioned in its pages. The story of God's dealings with His people can never grow old and more especially when such dealings affect the personal life. The article alluded to gave a most interesting account of the Shanghai Revival as its basis. Dr. Alexander Whyte, the great Scotch preacher and writer, remarks in his *Bible Characters* that St. Paul never tired of reciting the experience of his conversion on the Damascus road, an experience so vital and real as to live anew each time he told it. And so it is with all personal and truly Spirit-wrought experiences. As I read the account written by Mr. Loane I lived over again those days when we saw the Spirit work in mighty power. Within a very short time we received a copy of *The Shantung Revival*, sent by the author, Miss Mary Crawford, of the Southern Baptist Mission in China, an account of the Lord's dealings in revival which recorded as truly great miracles as the Apostles witnessed in the days after receiving the gift of Pentecost. We wrote to ask permission to use some parts of this blessed record of His working and received a glad consent.

But ere this reached us, we had received an answer to the query "What Next?" and at once began the collection of records of awakenings in different countries during this century. It was impressed upon us to issue a booklet giving the stories of revivals, beginning with the Revival in Wales in 1904–5. At once we wrote to our good friend, Mr. F. Kehl, to secure for us a copy of the story of the revival in the Khassia Hills, which followed the Welsh awakening. We already had the late Rev. R. B. Jones' *Rent Heavens*, and we also wished to procure a copy of the account of the great revival in Korea. We very soon found that it was no easy matter to get the material for a book such as we felt He would have us compile. The Rev. William Blair, author of *The Korean Pentecost*, was at the time in this country, and we appealed to him, only to receive a sympathetic reply but that he had no copy and doubted if one were in existence. Word came from Mr. Kehl enclosing a letter from Miss Thomas, a missionary to whom he had written, in which she said it was doubtful if a single copy of *The Khassia Revival* could be found, as it was now more than thirty years since the book was published. Nothing daunted, we began the compilation with such records as we had, praying that nothing of that which He desired should be missing when the book went to the printers.

The so-called "Nevius Method" is responsible under God for the truly wonderful growth of the Korean Church, paving the way for the outpouring of the

Spirit which took place soon after the Welsh Revival of 1904-5. In his very illuminating account of the Revival in Wales the late R. B. Jones says, "Though every revival ultimately culminates in a form which attracts the attention of all, no revival is of sudden origin. Behind the startling outburst is a process which sometimes goes on for years, a purifying and preparatory process. It was so in connection with that of 1904. Not many will care to contest that statement. It has already been hinted that the Revival goes back beyond November, 1904. Indeed, in most of the few records of the movement it is found that there were small burstings forth as early as February of that year."

Fleming H. Revell Co., New York publishers, very kindly granted us permission to use a brief account of the Revival in Korea included in a book, *The Korean Church and the Nevius Methods*, written by Dr. Clark, of the Northern Presbyterian Mission, and Mr. F. Kehl had consented to write of his recollections of things that happened during a visit he paid to the Khassia Hills when the revival was in progress. With these it *seemed* that we should have to be satisfied, but we constantly prayed with expectation, and He answered, though faith was severely tried, with the "exceeding abundantly above." Again we could only exclaim, "What hath God wrought!" Testimonies to the blessing this message brought, if we should attempt to reckon them up, are more than can be numbered. In March we had occasion to write to Mrs. Knox of the Southern Presbyterian Mission in Korea, and mentioned the matter of wanting a book on the Revival. Nothing happened until about the middle of May, when

Mrs. S. L. Roberts of Pyeng Yang, who until then was a total stranger to me, sent a copy of *The Korean Pentecost*, presumably the last to be preserved. My spirits rose, and prayer was intensified, for this was indeed a notable answer to prayer. With the material in hand we compiled a sizeable booklet, and yet we had no rest in our spirit—something was lacking, and He could supply it. We had rented our house for the months of July and August, and when the last week of June had come all was in order for flitting; then it was that we received from the Headquarters of the Welsh Presbyterian Mission in Liverpool a stained copy of *The Khassia Revival*. The Rev. J. Hughes Morris, Editorial Secretary of the Presbyterian Church of Wales, wrote that Miss Thomas, failing to locate a copy in India, had sent to the home office, and after a search the one and only copy had been found, and they were most happy to send it on, adding an apology for its worn condition. Needless to say, it looked perfectly lovely to me.

> " *God's plans like lilies, pure and white, unfold ;*
> *We must not force the close-shut leaves apart ;*
> *Time will reveal their calyxes of gold.*"

When *Calling to Remembrance* was issued, the first edition of twenty thousand was entirely exhausted within four months from the time it was announced that copies were available. They were sent out freely on the same conditions as all the books so far published. The one exception is our latest, *Revival in Romance and Realism*, for which we believe we should make a charge to meet such incidental expenses as providing funds for the translations, undertaken by men unable to finance the publications, and for the postage fund, which is no inconsiderable amount.

Some testimonies as to the fruit brought forth through this little message are appended herewith—

Mr. A. H. Maul, of "The Lord's Remembrancers," publishers of sound Gospel Tracts, Minneapolis, Minn.:

"We are so happy to receive your letter (December W.W.R.P.M.), telling of another edition of *Calling to Remembrance* being available. The one copy we have has been doing double and triple duty. I have had it bound in fine imitation leather, and it has gone the rounds in a Mission here and is now in a large Thursday afternoon prayer meeting. We feel that the little book is a modern supplement to the book of Acts. Would like to have one or more to send to pastors hungry for a Holy Ghost Revival. We know the Lord has and will continually bless you in this labour of love for our Lord and Saviour Jesus Christ."

A Southern pastor: "I have recently received a copy of your book, *Calling to Remembrance*, and have read it with much personal joy and blessing. It came just a week before I was to begin a meeting in my church. I had felt that we needed a new touch of the Divine Spirit as in other days, and this book proved to be a great help to me in my personal preparation. You might be interested to know that, while we went after a church revival and preached to the church at every service for two weeks, save four evangelistic sermons, that God blessed with some forty conversions just the same."

A pastor, Canada: "Your wonderful book, *Calling to Remembrance*, reached me some time ago. Thank you for it. The previous books were wonderful, but this one brought a greater message to me than all the rest. I have read portions of the book to my congregation. I want to read it over again and out of its contents group together a series of messages on *Revival*. Once again I thank you for your interest in a *World-Wide Revival*, and my prayer is that 1935 will be the most blessed year you have ever spent in His service down here (if He tarries)."

A friend in Colorado: "God has wonderfully blessed through the books that you so graciously sent at my request. The one to my old home kindled through prayer a spark for Revival, and a number were led to Christ, the power of prayer realized as never before in late years. Here God has been working and hearts have been stirred to pray. Groups are being led to unite for the outpouring of that blessing here and world-wide."

Thousands of prayer groups have resulted from the accounts given in the booklets disseminated, and friends constantly send lists of the names of others who are also revival-minded.

To the above letter was attached the names and addresses of four leaders, two Secretaries of Young People's Work, all of whom are in strategic positions of influence for the Master.

A minister in England: "I have been greatly stirred to prayer for revival by reading your booklet, *Calling to Remembrance*. I read portions of it to my prayer meeting of over two hundred Christians. We have been praying for revivals for some time, and the reading of your book in private and in public has stirred our hearts to greater intensity of longing and prayer. The need for revival is stupendous. I would very much like to obtain copies of *Power from on High* and *Calling to Remembrance*, for distribution amongst my prayer meeting members. I have tried Messrs. Marshall, Morgan & Scott, and they have none. The booklet came to my hand seemingly by chance, and I thank God for it."

> " *Saviour, Thy work revive !*
> *Here may we see*
>
> *Those who are dead in sin*
> *Quickened by Thee ;*
>
> *Come to our heart's delight,*
> *Make every burden light,*
>
> *Cheer Thou our waiting sight ;*
> *We long for Thee.*"

XX

WORLD-WIDE REVIVAL

U NDER this heading, *The Moody Monthly*, August, 1935, answered a question that seems to be agitating the minds of some (we are glad to say we believe they are comparatively few) of God's children. A correspondent of the "Question and Answer Department" asks: "Must 2 Thessalonians 2 : 3 take place before Christ returns to the earth? If so, are not our prayers for a world-wide revival in vain?" The editor, the late Dr. Gray, an ardent premillennialist, wisely and scripturally answered: "Yes, the apostasy here mentioned must be fulfilled prior to the *visible* return of Christ in power and glory to the earth. But since the Church and the Holy Spirit are still here, a world-wide revival is possible at any time the Church will meet the conditions. Sporadical and local revivals are occurring frequently, and we see no reason why a general revival of the Church should not be prayed for and expected at any time."

In the same month, *The Sunday School Times* of Philadelphia published a review of the World-Wide Revival Prayer Movement booklet, *Calling to Remembrance*:

"A study of the means and methods God uses to revive His Church and to make alive those who are dead in trespasses and sins, is the announced import of this third volume that has been issued by a widely-known movement to promote prayer for revival. It is a collection of soul-stirring incidents, some fresh from the foreign fields and others reprinted from books and periodicals, but all showing the mighty power of God and His willingness to meet and bless His people. There is searching power in the printed page, many incidents of conviction of sin, confession and restitution probing the heart deeply. One notable chapter deals with the great Welsh Revival of 1904. *The book is a call to Christians everywhere to pray until a great world-wide revival shall come."*

No one could think of Dr. Trumbell and his associates as being other than truly pre-millennial in their view-point. Such an endorsement of our purpose and way of promotion of our vision by these honoured men of God has been of inestimable value. It has been like Aaron and Hur when they held up the hands of Moses —if we may be pardoned for mentioning our humble efforts in the same category with theirs. But we believe that we too have been chosen for a specific ministry to the Church of Jesus Christ, to remind others of God's promises and the power of the Holy Spirit, for "Where there is no vision the people perish." The Rev. William Nicholson, a noted Irish evangelist, who has had the unique experience of going round the world no less than ten times in his evangelistic campaigns, has just written us a personal letter regarding those who consider a revival before the Lord's coming to be an impossibility, never I suppose dreaming that it would meet a need for this book about to go to the publishers. In his own vigorous language he says:

"I believe there is nothing quite so deadly as fundamentalism without the power and blessing of the Holy
Spirit. 'The *letter* killeth, it is the Spirit that makes
alive.' They are so strong on the *imputed* righteousness of Christ and don't mention the *imparted* righteousness which is the work of the Holy Spirit in every
believer's life. They seem to have the Lord dispensa-
tionalized to death. He can't do this, and He can't
do that, for this or that does not belong to this or that
dispensation. . . . When you talk about a revival that
will belt the globe and hasten and usher in the coming
again of our dear Lord Jesus, they say it can't be done
for it is not dispensational. I asked them here why it
was that the Lord gave me a revival that very day in
my own soul. If it were unscriptural, how was it I
got it? And if the Lord can and does that for me,
what is there to hinder Him from setting millions on
fire for Him and souls?"

One who has always held that the Second Coming
of the Lord was the next greatest event in the history
of the Church, wrote in response to our "Letter" of
December, 1935:

"The letter is a study, each section! A spiritual,
streamlined, Spirit-conditioned message, a non-stop to
the finish! All glory to God! 'He who speaks for
God has no other than God's message,' is said of
Moses when led back to the banks of the Nile and the
palaces of Memphis. May it not be now time to praise
for Revival, for answered prayer throughout the globe
wherever these prayer groups have been kindled into
Revival? This I have seen and rejoiced in. We are
but a 'little flock,' but a habitation of the Holy Spirit.
Then Habakkuk 2:3, 'The vision will surely come . . .

wait for it.' 'I will stand upon my watch, and set me upon the tower, and *look forth to see* what he will say unto me, and *what I shall answer*' (Hab. 2:1)—the Lord Himself depending upon our answer 'to prove us,' knowing Himself what He would do. And as the message goes forth, He will be listening for responses. So may it not now be time to praise for Revival? As I stated, I am praying for the 'World-Wide Revival' *now* going on in these hungry groups, many made hungry by the literature sent them, not seeing or expecting the old-fashioned way of revival."

In his latest little book, *A Revival is Coming*, Roger W. Babson, noted statistician, makes the confident prediction that "a great spiritual awakening is now ahead. All signs indicate that America will soon again be swept by a spiritual revival," etc. In a recent address Mr. Babson declared:

"Gambling is more rampant in this country to-day than ever before in its history. A billion dollars changed hands during 1935 in horse racing, dog racing, slot machines, and so forth. The liquor business and all forms of questionable amusements have been booming as never before. This has increased the figures on bank clearings and made us appear prosperous. This activity, however, has done nothing to improve the standard of living, but rather, has tended to reduce the standard of living."

Though Mr. Babson and I do not arrive at our convictions of an expectation of a revival by precisely the same route, I am fully convinced that God is soon to visit His people with an outpouring of Holy Ghost power in answer to His people's prayers. "It is time,

Lord, for thee to work, for they have made void thy law." When this time of refreshing comes, the "dead bones" that now occupy space in the churches will be clothed with the Spirit, and learn, for the first time probably, to stand upon their own spiritual feet, and contribute to the life of the Church, instead of leaving to the pastor the sacred ministry of prayer and preaching. The result will be an ingathering of souls such as has never been known in all the history of the Church Militant and Triumphant.

A missionary in the jungles of India tells what happened there during the Khassia Revival. She writes:

"What would you think of a big market and bazaar deserted at the busiest hour of the day, all buying and selling at a standstill, whilst the people flocked to hear the preaching of the Gospel at an open-air service nearby? And the power that brought them there kept them listening spell-bound, as they learned the way of salvation from the lips of a simple village teacher, until from many hearts in that crowd the cry went up, 'What must we do to be saved?' Women were there who were liquor-sellers. They returned to their stalls in the market only to pour out their liquor on the ground, and then hastened away to their homes in order to destroy all trace of its manufacture there, although it was their only means of livelihood. After cleansing their houses, they came at night to the meeting in the little schoolhouse and offered themselves and their families to the Lord. . . . We commenced work in a village there six years ago, and sent a teacher to live there, but oh, it was hopeless work, not a Christian in the whole place for a long time, and only a few little children coming for instruction. It seemed to be time, strength and money wasted, no sign of a blessing. But the time, God's time, had not come; now it has. One Sunday morning at daybreak the teacher was awakened by the sound of singing in the schoolroom, and on going in found it as full as it would hold of men, women and children, all singing heartily one of the hymns he had been labouring to teach them for months. Now they were singing with all their hearts—hearts in which the Holy Spirit was working mightily. Soon there was a great outburst of prayer, cries for pardon and praise for sins forgiven. The meeting continued all day and all the following night, and I do not know whether it is finished yet or not. But this we know, that not only in that village but in villages around the Lord is adding to the Church daily such as shall be saved."

"That the world may know" was the burden of our Lord's prayer as recorded in the seventeenth chapter of the Gospel of St. John; and surely this prayer is being answered through the intercession of His own elect to an extent, and in ways not conceived of by flesh and blood. Again the great land of India is being shaken by the Spirit of the living God, as extracts from letters which follow clearly prove. A missionary writes:

"Not only the biggest thing in the history of missions, but in the whole history of the Church, confronts us to-day, in the vast movement of India's Outcastes. It would not be wise to make known all facts, publicly, which allow us to say with confidence that these seventy millions are heading toward Christ; but still it is so much of a certainty that we can say that in the whole history of the Christian Church there has

DR. HENRY M. WOODS,
SUMMER, 1932

INDIA THE OBJECTIVE: ON BOARD
S.S. "WINIFREDIAN," WITH MRS. KIRK,
AUGUST, 1921

[*Face page* 214

never before been such an open door for winning millions to Christ. . . . Throughout India to-day, to the ears of faith, there is a 'going in the tops of the mulberry trees.' The sleep of death that has held souls through many generations is being shaken. . . . It is in response to the 'going' that the call from the Word of God comes to the Christian Church: 'Bestir thyself, for the Lord is gone out before thee.' This is *the great opportunity* for all members of the Church of Christ to concentrate in prayer and effort, that these seekers after a better life than the one they have lived so far may be shown the way to Eternal Life. We would ask, most earnestly, our faithful prayer-helpers to meet at the Throne of Grace on behalf of this oppressed people, who have been taught that the holy things of God are *not for low castes and women*. . . . Pray that the drawing power of the Cross of Christ may work mightily, and that souls may bow before Him in absolute yieldedness and consecration of spirit, soul, and body, so that they may find Life that is life indeed and a new era will begin in India."

From other sources we learn more of the marvels of His grace to a despised and down-trodden class of people who, as individuals, their very shadow falling upon one of a higher station in life is considered polluting:

"Since last writing the Depressed Classes have met, in Conference, in Lucknow. Their leader is Dr. Ambedkar, a brilliant lawyer, a doctor of philosophy in English, German, and American universities, and a wonderful organizer. Though he was not well enough to be present at Lucknow, they passed a resolution unanimously endorsing his policy, and pledging themselves to follow his lead absolutely. A second resolution committed them to the repudiation of Hinduism and all its oppression; while a third resolution relegated to another year's conference the choice of a new religion to take the place of the old Hinduism. Under the old system, unchanged for centuries, these sixty millions have never been allowed to do anything but the most menial duties, duties which the Caste people felt to be altogether beneath them; they were not allowed to eat with the Caste people, nor to use the same wells; and, of course, never to intermarry. How impossible it seemed to change a thraldom like this! As one looks back, one sees God's servants, the missionaries, obeying His command, and fearlessly proclaiming a free salvation to all, by simple faith in Christ's atoning work on the Cross. Converts stepped out and followed their Saviour, refusing to worship idols which were closely interwoven with every detail of their life and daily work. . . . A new joy had come into their lives, through the consciousness of sin forgiven; self-respect began to grow, and then a desire for education. After a time, education opened the doors of the universities, and the Outcastes found themselves the equals of the Caste people, and sought for, and obtained Government appointments, and now, in many cases, the Brahmins themselves have to apply to them for permits, etc.

"Everywhere the Depressed Classes are bestirring themselves. *Over enormous areas, if a vote were taken to-day, as to the religion which should be adopted, an overwhelming majority would vote for Christianity.* Voting for a national religion will not make men *new creatures in Christ Jesus*—millions have no idea what it means to live as Christians. One Indian paper states that the present stream of conversions to Christianity from the Untouchables is, at least, 15,000 per month, and that it may increase till 300,000 a year are pouring into the Christian Church. A tremendous responsibility to the Christian Church—the followers of Christ! Who is going to teach these converts the elementary truths of the Christian life? *How few the missionaries are for the task that confronts them.* Undoubtedly, God is behind these mighty changes, and one wonders if He is not about to call out many of these poor, despised Untouchables, and then fill them with His Spirit, that they may be *the reapers* on a scale never dreamt of by us. *Let* us pray much, for only He knows the true solution."

From another letter we quote the following, regarding the native State of Travancore:

"Have you heard that a group of people in the south of India are wanting to come over, *as a people*, to Christianity? They number over three millions, I think it is, and they are just outside the Caste System, and so are refused entrance into the temples, and the use of wells, etc. . . . This is happening in the Native State of Travancore, and, of course, the authorities are rather scared. Travancore is a Hindu State, and has a Hindu Ruler, but, if these people do become Christians, it will become a Christian State! *The Christians of the District are rising up and taking their part in evangelizing the villages*, and in the northern part of the State Syrian Christians are busy, too. It is a great opportunity, and although many of the people are coming in for what they can get, and for a recognized position in the community life, there are many, too, who are seeking for light, and for *the Truth*. The pity of it all is, that the churches have not enough workers to cope with these vast numbers. Would it not be a wonderful thing to have a Christian State in India? All through *the south of India*, they seem to be having seasons of revival, and blessing among the Christians themselves, and they are beginning to *see the need of* the unevangelized ones, and in one mission where they have had very few converts in the ninety years of their work there, *now they are having thousands in a year, and the numbers are growing.*"

May God raise up many, many *intercessors* at this time, *to stand before Him, for His purposes to be accomplished*, and the *bondage of Satan to be broken* over the millions of precious souls in India (perhaps the land most tightly bound to Satan's thralls of any upon earth). May the Lord Jesus see of the travail of His soul, *through the members of His Body*, and have a rich inheritance from that benighted land!

What is greatly needed is *a large force of missionaries* to lead this great company of new adherents to the religion of Jesus Christ.

"INSTEAD"

Isaiah 55 : 13

" *Instead of the thorn there shall come up the fir tree,*
  Instead of the brier, the myrtle shall spring,
 Back to its primeval freshness and beauty,
 God will creation triumphantly bring.

" *Streams in the desert shall heal the parched places,*
  The rose in the wilderness, fragrance shall shed ;
 The mountains and hills shall break forth in praises,
 Wonderful word of Jehovah, ' Instead.'

" Alone in the Garden while others are sleeping,
The sinless Redeemer a suppliant kneels.
His earnest entreaty, His blood-drops, His weeping,
To the heart of the Father, His anguish reveals.

"'Tho' bitter the cup, that Surety has taken,
'Tho' heavy the stroke that must fall on His head,
He goes to the cross, to be cursed and forsaken,
To give us the cup of salvation, instead.

" Believer, rejoice, for the glad day is nearing,
For which all creation still travails in pain ;
When Christ our Redeemer, in glory appearing,
Shall take to Himself His great power and reign.

" When Satan the evil usurper expelling,
To earth's farthest limits, His Kingdom shall spread.
And peace and prosperity, sweetly be telling,
That Jesus Emmanuel ruleth, ' Instead.' "

—R. W. Cowdery.

(Isa. 11 and Isa. 35.)

We add an article entitled, "How to Secure a Genuine Revival," from the pen of Dr. Egbert W. Smith, Field Secretary of the Presbyterian Committee of Foreign Missions. Dr. Smith wrote us on March 26, 1936: "I shall be delighted to have you use that article in any way you see fit, and I shall certainly pray that whatever use you may make of it may be blessed of God to the spread of the revival spirit." His article follows:

"For several years our Church has been seeking a revival. It has tried all kinds of methods. But the revival has not come. The following account of a great and genuine revival at our Lubondai station in the Congo presents, it seems to me, the one, the true, the infalliable method of securing a revival. It is well worth reading by every minister and every member of our Church. The following account is given by Mr. William J. Anderson, of Lubondai:

"'For the last two years the Spirit of the Lord has been working among us in a way never experienced before. The word revival might be used, but that word has been almost worked to death. It all began with us, the missionaries. After months of earnest prayer, we found ourselves all of one mind, burdened for a fresh outpouring of the Holy Spirit. Our testimony seemed to be fruitless. We seemed to be bucking against an invisible but impenetrable wall. The enemy seemed to be on the upper hand. So we got together, set apart a week—or as long as it might take—and humbled ourselves in the dust before our God. We spared not ourselves. We were determined that if there was anything in our lives blocking the working of the Holy Spirit, then, God helping us, it should be done away with. God revealed a number of things. They were made right. When this was done, and we held back nothing, but surrendered all to Him, then God's blessing came. Peace, joy, fellowship, power, such as we had never experienced before.

"'We witnessed to the leaders among the natives. Then to the evangelists. The Spirit seized them too. Such confession of sin! Weeping, completely broken down, on their knees, some with their faces in the dust. It spread to the workmen, to nearby villages. All hours of the day and night they came, under great conviction of sin, wanting to get right with God. And such changed lives as we saw! Here was a man, a carpenter, had beat his wife several times, wanted to get rid of her and marry another, has just about broken up the work in the carpenter shop by trying to involve others in the shop in the palaver. But now, it was a joy to step into the shop. You could feel the difference. It was a pleasure to work with them.

"'So it spread. Volumes could be filled, citing case after case. Those transformed evangelists went back to their villages, witnessed and preached as never before in their lives. And what are the results? The tide was turned. The wall was broken down. People began seeking the Lord by the score, then by the hundred. Chiefs, old men and women—three classes that heretofore had showed practically no interest in the Gospel—were brought under conviction, confessed their sins, and got right with God. Last year there were over two thousand baptized in this one territory. It looks as if there will be more than that this year. Villages that, a couple of years ago, were most offensive to visiting missionaries, and most antagonistic to the Gospel, have since sent begging to have us establish work in their midst. They want teachers (evangelists). They want to learn about God. Delegations come in by the score. They plead. They beg. They want an evangelist to take back right away, to live among them and teach them the Way of God. Right now we have at least one hundred and fifty more calls for evangelists than we can meet. And that is in just this one territory of Lubondai.'"

What changes will take place in governmental affairs as well as in every department of life when men turn to God. The curse of drink will then disappear, gambling and other forms of vice will cease. Then let us pray without ceasing, until power from on high is released and souls held in the awful bondage of Satan are delivered.

God is, and has been, preparing the way for a manifestation of His power, a manifestation which none can gainsay or resist. The stories told in this little volume of parishes and churches revived, prayer groups multiplying—what else can be meant than that these things are the precursor of the blessing promised if we meet the condition: "Bring ye all the tithes into the storehouse, that there may be meat in mine house, and prove me now herewith, saith the Lord of hosts, if I will not open you the windows of heaven, and pour you out a blessing, that there shall not be room enough to receive it" (Malachi 3: 10).

Wonderful are the ways of God! Little did we realize that the seven years spent in foreign countries, becoming acquainted in our unhurried travels with conditions at close range, were furnishing the basis for the extensive operations of a work that would encircle the globe. Many years ago the Holy Spirit implanted in my mind the words: "I am the Lord thy God which teacheth thee to profit, which leadeth thee by the way that thou shouldest go." And while at the time we were yet without understanding of their full meaning, in His time we were compelled to see that He had all the years been planning the way that He would lead us and prepare us to follow on to know His will.

> "*His way may lead through darkness, but it leads to light at last.*"

Some six or more years ago, the sponsors of the World-Wide Revival Prayer Movement made a wide distribution—especially among university and college students—of a book, *Hudson Taylor, the Man That*

Believed God, the biography of one of the great missionary-statesmen of the present generation. In this effort we had the co-operation of leaders in Christian work in all parts of the world, Canada, New Zealand, Australia, Great Britain and the United States. The result of this "broadcast" was altogether encouraging and stimulating and furnished an army of new recruits for work in the "regions beyond." This is described in Ch. XIII, "How It Happened."

Believing that we have been guided by the Holy Spirit in the selection of another great record of missionary achievement in the book, *The Life of C. T. Studd*, which in our estimation is without a peer—for the purpose intended, and which tells the story of more than forty years of unremitting sacrifice and hardship —paralleling more nearly the life of the Apostle Paul in this respect than any other of which we know—we launch a new offensive against the forces of evil in the challenge the book holds for young men and women. The great Earl Haig said during the late World War, "The most effective defence consists of a vigorous attack upon the enemy." We believe the message of this book is suited for just such a task; more than that, we believe it will be mightily used of God in the pulling down of the strongholds of Satan wherever and by whomsoever it may be read. We hope, with the help of friends in strategic positions, presidents of universities and colleges and their colleagues, to reach students and enlist them in the greatest of all active service, that of unfurling the blood-stained flag of the Cross where His name is not yet known. This effort has been undertaken after much patient and prolonged prayer, and will be followed with watching and constant remembrance of the great objective which motivated this another "Forward Movement" for the whole Church of which Jesus Christ is the glorious Head and the Holy Spirit the Administrator of its affairs.

In *The Life of C. T. Studd* the author, Norman P. Grubb, son-in-law and co-worker of "C.T.," gives a masterly review of the events in the life of this remarkable man—culminating in his greatest achievement, the founding of the Worldwide Evangelization Crusade. Through this God-inspired medium the Gospel of redeeming grace has been carried to thousands who heretofore, helpless and hopeless, are now coming to know Him, whom to know is life eternal. With thanksgiving to those who have so selflessly shared in making this distribution possible, we launch this effort—with prayer following every copy of the edition.